INNER CHILD CARDS
WORKBOOK

Inner Child Cards Workbook

FURTHER EXERCISES AND MYSTICAL
TEACHINGS FROM THE FAIRY-TALE TAROT

ISHA LERNER

ILLUSTRATED BY CHRISTOPHER GUILFOIL

Bear & Company
Rochester, Vermont

Bear & Company
One Park Street
Rochester, Vermont 05767
www.InnerTraditions.com

Bear & Company is a division of Inner Traditions International

Library of Congress Cataloging-in-Publication Data

Lerner, Isha, 1954-
  The inner child cards workbook : further exercises and mystical teachings from the fairy-tale tarot / Isha Lerner.
      p. cm.
Includes bibliographical references.
  ISBN 1-879181-89-4
  1. Tarot. 2. Fairy tales—Miscellanea. I. Title.
  BF1879.T2 L436 2002
  133.3'2424—dc21
                                        2002005755

Printed and bound in the United States at Lake Book

10 9 8 7 6 5 4 3 2 1

Text design and layout by Mary Anne Hurhula
This book was typeset in Goudy with Delphin as display typeface

For my sister Christeen who walked the path of childhood with me—carnation song, mud pies, shadows on the wall, Dodie's laughter in the morning, and Mom's lemon cake—I can only share these memories with you.

Contents

Acknowledgments   ix

Introduction: Fairy Tales and the Odyssey of the Human Soul   1

CHAPTER 1: The Feminine in Fairy Tales   7

    Both Good and Evil Characters Are Ultimately Good   9

    The Feminine Nature of Fairy Tales   13

    Each Character Is a Different Aspect of One's Own Psyche,

        Seeking Wholeness Through Alchemical Marriage   15

CHAPTER 2: Initiation, Enchantment, and Awakening   18

    Initiation: Corresponding to the Alchemical Stage

        of Melanosis   21

    Enchantment: Corresponding to the Alchemical Stage

        of Leukosis   22

    Awakening: Corresponding to the Alchemical Stages

        of Xanthosis and Iosis   23

CHAPTER 3: The Archetypes of the Soul and Karmic Imprints   25

    Fairy Tales: Liberators of the Soul   26

    Karmic Imprints   28

    Fairy-Tale Symbolism Replenishes the Soul   33

CHAPTER 4: Fairy-Tale Mysticism and the Major Arcana   38

Tarot and Fairy Tales: Branches on the Tree
    of Ancient Knowledge   38

The Major Arcana: A Cyclical Journey of Transformation 42

CHAPTER 5: Mirrors to Humanity   45

The Trumps: The Soul's Journey   46

The Court Cards: Magic Mirrors   49

The Numerical Cards: Everyday Encounters   52

CHAPTER 6: Additional Ways to Use the *Inner Child Cards*   56

Past-Life Regression   57

Dreamwork   60

Inner Child Cards Rummy   61

CHAPTER 7: New Layouts   63

The Dynamic Star Layout   63

The Rebirth Layout   65

The Archetype Layout: Mirror, Mirror on the Wall   67

The Yellow Brick Road Layout   69

CHAPTER 8: The Twenty-Two Major Arcana   72

0 • Little Red Cap: The Fool   74

I • Aladdin and the Magic Lamp: The Magician   76

II • The Fairy Godmother: The High Priestess   79

III • Mother Goose: The Empress   81

IV • The Emperor's New Clothes: The Emperor   83

V • The Wizard: The Hierophant   86

VI • Hansel and Gretel: The Lovers   89

VII • Peter Pan: The Chariot   92

VIII • Beauty and the Beast: Strength   94

IX • Snow White: The Hermit   97

X • Alice in Wonderland: The Wheel of Fortune   99

XI • The Midas Touch: Justice   102

XII • Jack and the Beanstalk: The Hanged One   105

XIII • Sleeping Beauty: Death   108

XIV • The Guardian Angel: Temperance   111

XV • The Big Bad Wolf: The Devil   113

XVI • Rapunzel: The Tower   115

XVII • Wishing Upon a Star: The Star   117

XVIII • Cinderella: The Moon   119

XIX • The Yellow Brick Road: The Sun   122

XX • The Three Little Pigs: Judgment   125

XXI • The Earth Child: The World   128

CHAPTER 9: The Minor Arcana   130

The Magic Wands   132

The Swords of Truth   155

The Winged Hearts   181

The Earth Crystals   199

Bibliography   226

Acknowledgments

A warm and heart-felt thank you to: Tara McKinney for her skillful editing and endless support; Mark Lerner, the coauthor of *Inner Child Cards: A Fairy-Tale Tarot,* who served as a beacon of light at the end of the tunnel; my youngest daughter Sophie, who had a very busy mom and was a tremendous sport about it; Michael, for good humor and high spirits; and, of course, the great people at Inner Traditions International • Bear & Company, especially my editor, Laura Schlivek.

Introduction

Fairy Tales and the Odyssey of the Human Soul

Welcome to the *Inner Child Cards Workbook*. It has been a long-held dream of mine to offer an intensive book and study guide on the mystical properties of fairy tales and tarot. I have found that once people comprehend the true meaning of fairy-tale symbolism, they are able to unlock a very special treasure that has been with them since childhood and strengthen the relationship they have with their inner life. Many people attending my classes on the use of *Inner Child Cards: A Fairy-Tale Tarot* over the past nine years have encouraged me to write a companion book, one that would serve as a workbook and guide to help them explore the material in that book further. This current effort is the culmination of ten years of study and research.

The *Inner Child Cards Workbook* is designed to educate and inform as well as to serve as an interactive resource book with *Inner Child Cards*. It also stands very well on its own—those who do not own *Inner Child Cards* may use it as a stepping stone toward a greater awareness of fairy tales, the tarot, and alchemy. Those who own *Inner Child Cards* may use it as an additional reference for their work with the cards, as well as to enhance their understanding of tarot and fairy tales. I have woven new material on the archetypal meaning of fairy tales into a workbook format, offering the individual a deeply mystical and profoundly therapeutic journey through fairy-tale symbolism. The *Inner Child Cards Workbook* offers new card layouts, teaches new divination methods, and offers a series of personal growth exercises that correspond to each Major Arcana card, including visualizations, affirmations, questions, and suggested ways one can actualize the fairy-tale teachings in one's life.

In 1990, while in the midst of writing *Inner Child Cards: A Fairy-Tale Tarot*, I found myself cleaning the attic of my childhood home after my mother had passed away. In an old box of saved treasures, I discovered a book entitled *The Very Tall Book of Fairy Tales*. As a child, I had loved this book that my great-aunt had sent to me from England, and I had marked the tales that were my favorites with a check mark. Later in life, I had experienced the healing effect of researching and gaining new understanding about the deeper meaning of those tales that had touched my heart and soul as a child.

That same box contained a story I had written at the age of seven called "Buffy the Blind Man's Dog," which clearly identified patterns I was living out and seeking to understand at the time. In the first chapter, the blind man's dog gets killed by a reckless driver. The saga explores the issues of survival, truth, and healing. I was very moved to find this story and, in the revisiting of it, was able to gain a tremendous amount of compassion for my own healing journey. The experience taught me the power of first writing one's own story and then looking back upon that story with a measure of detachment, as if it were a fairy tale.

My lectures and workshops on *Inner Child Cards* have led me to conclude that many people are now ready to grasp the deeper meaning of "childhood stories"—whether their own or others—and to glean from them their true mystical teachings. Of the various aspects of our collective memory and childhood imprint, the fairy tale has widely served to open the door to a vast world of imagination and dream. Identifying the stories that were important to us as children helps us to highlight the resonant themes in our own lives and also gives us strength. We are reminded that the quest for individuation is a universal matter, and that we all encounter certain difficult challenges and stages of initiation. In an archetypal way, fairy tales lay bare the vast territory of the soul. Our quest for a full human existence requires that we embrace and integrate all aspects of human development into our daily lives, even those involving suffering, abandonment, and fear. If we listen with our hearts and are receptive to the magic of the story, we come face to face with the beautiful essence of our own life's journey.

My life has been transformed through the process of delving deeply into the mystical meaning of fairy tales. As I've applied the insights gleaned in this way to my own circumstances and life passages, I have found the pathway to my destiny cleared. Looking deeply into my own suffering and fear, I, like many fairy-tale protagonists, have pushed forward into the unknown, entered the depths of my own soul's journey, and found solace in the stages of progress toward maturation and truth.

For example, as you will see in the *Workbook*, the story of "Little Red Cap" is a mystical exploration of the process of individuation and increasing freedom. Little Red Riding Hood is one of the few main fairy-tale characters endowed with a loving mother who cares for her and watches over her. Her proverbial red cap is a symbol of her innate wish to be enlightened and awakened to the greater wisdom of the world. She must meet the wolf—symbolizing the shadow of her past, her fears, and her dark side—and undergo the initiation he brings to her as he attempts to fool her and devour her unformed wisdom. This is the part of herself that must be found and brought to consciousness.

Little Red Cap journeys to grandmother's house, the ancestral cottage of transformation, where she learns about the deceptive side of life—the wolf dressed as grandmother. She is eventually graced with enlightenment and rebirth when the woodsman cuts open the belly of the wolf and sets her free. Ultimately, she is awakened to a new level of being as she learns to outsmart the Big Bad Wolf and meet the many challenges life has set before her.

In some essential way, we are all Little Red Cap and her story is our story. So, if what you're looking for is a better understanding of yourself and your story—in the context of fairy-tale mysticism and universality—then you've come to the right place. What follows is your story, told in magical, poetic, epic terms with a grand cast of characters, all of which are different aspects of you!

The first three chapters of the *Inner Child Cards Workbook* contain a distillation of many years of lecture, class, and workshop material. People's questions and observations about fairy tales, mythology, mysticism, and tarot—which have been shared with me during my travels and public sharings—are incorporated into the manuscript. I have pieced together a fabric of these questions and intuitive inquiries with years of my own research and hands-on encounters with *Inner Child Cards* in order to create a mythical journey for the soul.

The fourth and fifth chapters offer a look at the tarot and its connection to fairy-tale mysticism and the power of numbers. I feel it is important for the student of tarot and *Inner Child Cards* to understand the significance of numbers in tarot and stories. They serve as symbolic codes and messages throughout stories just as the number on a tarot card offers information about the deeper meaning of the card. Chapter Six is devoted to offering new and exciting ways to use the *Inner Child Cards*, including past-life regression, dreamwork, and even a card game. Chapter Seven offers several new layouts for readings of *Inner Child Cards*, including The Dynamic Star layout and The Yellow Brick Road layout.

The remaining two chapters offer individual descriptions of each *Inner Child Card*—including questions, affirmations, and quotations.

This information complements that given in the book that accompanies the *Inner Child Cards*. Both books are designed to be an asset for the layperson who is eager to learn how to interpret the cards with confidence and ease. Whether an individual prefers to choose one card as a message for the soul or lay out a complete spread, the intention of this book is to deepen one's experience with tarot, fairy tales, and symbolic therapy work.

It is my greatest pleasure to share the mystical language of fairy-tale lore and tarot with the world. My wish to create this book has been granted, with the support and guidance of Inner Traditions • Bear and Company. I hope it will inspire and ignite the creative forces of love and wisdom for each person who opens its pages. Love Heals All.

Chapter 1

The Feminine in Fairy Tales

Over time, we have seen the feminine instinctive nature looted, driven back, and overbuilt. For long periods it has been mismanaged like the wildlife and the wildlands. For several thousand years, as soon and as often as we turn our backs, it is relegated to the poorest land in the psyche. The spiritual lands of Wild Woman have, throughout history, been plundered or burnt, dens bulldozed, and natural cycles forced into unnatural rhythms to please others.

—Clarissa Pinkola Estes,
Women Who Run with the Wolves

Many feminists—along with conscientious mothers and fathers who came of age during the 1960s and 1970s—have expressed serious reservations about the sex-role content of fairy tales. Some have even found them wholly unsuitable for their children due to characters like the evil witch who eats little children. Indeed, these characters, if misunderstood, will conjure up negative images and projections. I wrestled with this problem myself.

My three daughters are the most precious jewels I have uncovered in this lifetime. I want nothing more than for each of them to be free of self-negating thoughts about their bodies, intelligence, and self-worth. When my first two daughters were very young, I felt a need to protect them from the frightening images of the enchantress found in fairy tales, for I wanted them to think of witches as good. On the other end of the spectrum, I shied away from characters like Cinderella and Snow White, which seemed to perpetuate the cult of romantic idealism and feminine passivity into which I had been indoctrinated as a child. I wanted to protect my girls from the heart-breaking process of first building up romantic illusions and then having them shattered. I wanted them to be strong and self-reliant. Clearly, I wasn't happy with fairy tales, but, at the same time, I loved them and wanted to know more about them.

I first encountered the idea that a fairy tale could have a mystical dimension that represented the unfolding of the soul in 1984 when my husband Mark and I enrolled our young daughters Gabrielle and Katya in the Waldorf School system, founded by Rudolf Steiner. Steiner was an Austrian mystic, scientist, and scholar whose writings, teachings, and lectures have inspired the world to explore the vast territories of the soul and spirit.

During my years at the Findhorn Foundation in Scotland, I had been exposed to Steiner's work. I first learned of the existence of an educational system that carried his philosophy into the world through other Findhorn community members with small children. Throughout his life, Rudolf Steiner worked on the articulation of a path of inner schooling capable of providing a person with a well-rounded, scientifically grounded knowledge of spiritual realities. As my husband and I became acquainted with the Waldorf School program, we discovered that fairy tales are presented as part of the class curriculum in each grade and are chosen carefully according to each child's maturation cycle and inner soul development.

My young heart, exuberant and committed to the unfolding beauty of my daughters, questioned some of the content of the stories, which led me into discussions and research regarding the lore, history, and deeper meaning of fairy tales. With the help of astute teachers at the school followed by many years of my own studies, I have come to understand the mystical quality of the tales that have become such a part of my everyday life. Today, as I integrate the tales into my work by combining fairy-tale archetypes with astrology, tarot, mythology, and therapy work, I am in awe of the power of these magical stories to stir the soul.

As I began to relate to fairy tales on a mystical level, my concerns about their stereotypical portrayal of women began to dissolve. The following three insights have gradually washed away my reservations and concerns: 1) despite superficial appearances to the contrary, both good and evil characters are, ultimately, good; 2) fairy tales are inherently feminine in nature; and 3) all characters in any given fairy tale are different aspects of one's own psyche, seeking wholeness through alchemical marriage. Let us explore each of these insights in turn.

BOTH GOOD AND EVIL CHARACTERS ARE ULTIMATELY GOOD

Often characters that appear helpless, self-sacrificing, and unrealistically sweet and pure are cast as female, typically as maidens, fairies, mermaids, orphan girls, and so on. In many of the most popular fairy tales, a saintly woman gives birth to a beautiful child, most often a girl, who has the virtues of goodness and purity. At the very beginning of the tale, the mother typically dies, leaving the young child in her father's care, and eventually at the mercy of a mean and cruel stepmother. The core message of this story line is that we all come from goodness and that our inherent goodness can never be taken from us, even as we wander lost in the forest, encountering harsh and difficult obstacles along the way.

In cosmological terms, the saintly mother of fairy-tale lore represents the Great Goddess, the Mother of the World. In Egyptian mythology, she is known as Isis, whose vessel was the golden chalice that birthed the Sun and the Moon. In the context of mystical Christianity, she is the Queen of Heaven, the Holy Madonna, whose body births the Christ Child, symbolizing the part of our inner psyche that carries ego consciousness forward toward true individuation and higher service. She may also be Venus, The Empress—Trump number III of the tarot—representing the all-loving incarnation into an earthly body. Her body is sacred, and her offspring can be nothing less than the miraculous fulfillment of her own divinity.

Within the context of the fairy tale, the death of the good mother teaches us that in order to rise to higher consciousness we must first be cut free of the heavenly umbilical cord that has nurtured our soul. In this way, we experience the full impact of our karmic situation here on earth. Within this crucible we are compelled to undertake a sacred quest for wholeness and freedom. A poignant illustration of this is the fact that a majority of women's rights activists at the turn of the century had lost their mothers early in life. This is not to suggest that the presence of a stable and secure mother will necessarily stunt one's growth. However, it does point to the virtue of finding one's own strength amidst hardship. When a child has been left motherless, in the earthly sense, she cannot rest until she finds her way back to her true spiritual home, the only true resting place. Such yearning and heartache is therefore a great gift—perhaps the greatest gift of all.

On the other hand, when the mother is present in the lives of her children, she is wise to let go of them in appropriate ways through the various developmental stages so that they may cultivate their own courage and strength. One way or another, we all eventually strive for self-realization. The feminine in fairy tales illuminates this process. Our journey on this planet is moist and fertile, offering many opportunities to discover our own worth, creativity, and love. We are destined to retrieve our own riches, but first we must earn our way back home. There we will meet the reward of our suffering and service. This is not to say that life on earth must be difficult. However, there are lessons to be learned along the way, and we often forget that we can never really be separated from the unconditional, eternal love of the Great Mother who birthed us all.

In our forgetting, we must all face the fearful terrain of darkness, the underworld, where dragons and scary things reside. The dark side of the feminine is expressed mythologically through characters such as the cruel stepmother, the wicked witch, the imperious queen, and the like. We need this part, as well, in order to be whole. As Clarissa Pinkola Estes explains in her stunning book *Women Who Run with the Wolves*,

> The wise woman is also known as "the woman who lives at the end of time," or the "woman who lives at the edge of the world." And this criatura is always a creator-hag, or a death goddess, or a maiden in descent, or any other number of personifications. She is both friend and mother to all those who have lost their way, all those who need a learning, all those who have a riddle to solve, all those out in the forest or the desert wandering and searching.*

Once the golden umbilical cord of the Heavenly Mother has been cut, it is the umbilical of the Dark Mother that connects us to the temporal world. As already mentioned, she is often the catalyst

*Clarissa Pinkola Estes, *Women Who Run with the Wolves* (New York: Ballantine Books, 1992).

who prompts our growth and search for greater meaning within the earthly realm.*

In cosmological terms, the Dark Mother has taken many forms around the planet. In India, she is known as Shakti or Mother Kali. In the Christian world, she appears as a dark form of the Virgin Mary known as the Black Madonna. In the Tibetan Buddhist pantheon she has many manifestations, among them Vajrayogini and dark forms of the Buddha Tara. All such manifestations of the Dark Mother invite us into the luminous darkness in order to experience the transformation awaiting our souls.

The fairy tale enchantress, or wicked witch, casts the spell that will be the source of the child's life initiation. If Snow White had not been abandoned to the deep, dark woods by her jealous stepmother, she would not have found the cottage that served as her stepping-stone toward self-actualization. The dark is vital; it is the fertile ground that sprouts our seeds, allowing for the gestation of that which is yet to come. It is from the dark star-lit heaven that the luminescent Moon shines forth, lighting the pathways of our destiny. The Moon, the manna, the matrix, and the womb are aspects of the Dark Mother transforming. The dark forces in our old stories suggest that there is work to be done and initiation to take place. A renewal of the soul and a resurrection of some sort are imminent.

---

*It is interesting to note that oftentimes the offspring of the cruel stepmother are themselves mean and cruel. These sisters, as in Cinderella, have not been set free to explore the depths of their individuation. They are tethered to the root of the Dark Mother in unhealthy ways that do not allow for resolution with the light. Even they may eventually find their way home, however. Perhaps they will experience a fated time in their own incarnation cycles when they, too, will be propelled into the quest for wholeness and freedom.

THE FEMININE NATURE OF FAIRY TALES

Fairy tales are, by nature, feminine. I refer to the feminine as an aspect of human consciousness, male or female, which is in harmonic relationship with the cosmology of nature, the cosmos, and all of life. Ultimately, the essence of the "Divine Feminine" is eternal, loving, and fertile and serves as a source of inspiration that stirs the soul toward creation and transformation. Fairy tales invoke this essence within the heart of humanity. What is more, they embody both "good" and "evil" expressions of the feminine, in the sense that they gently nurture and support our growth, on the one hand, and can also serve as rather ruthless catalysts for growth when necessary, on the other. They are like the two faces of the Tibetan Goddess Tara: the white form, which is infinitely patient and yielding in her compassion; and the dark form, which appears wrathful because, in her fierce compassion, she is willing to do whatever it takes to wake us up. The pure energy of wrath is simply that which propels us forward when we are stuck. Essentially, it is the raw energy of the mother pushing us through the birth canal.

Water is a powerful symbol of transformation in many fairy tales. Again, we notice a merging with that which is of the womb, the mysterious, the unseen. Fairy tales are not dry; they are moist. This moisture is found in the caverns of the dark earth and the crystal dew on the morning violets. The tears—the moisture of the soul—of Beauty in "Beauty and the Beast" and of Rapunzel are restorative, bringing back the handsome form or the sight of the beloved prince. King Midas can only undo his curse of greed if he will dive into a pool and pour water from a special vase over all that he has turned to gold. The wicked witch in *The Wizard of Oz* is finally defeated by water. Hansel and Gretel cannot reach their true home unless they cross the water on the back of a white swan. In many old fairy tales, we find a talking frog, an amphibious creature that dwells near water. This being is often magical. In fact, it is often the prince in disguise. The list goes on and on, affirming the one important point I wish to make—fairy tales are feminine by nature and all that is dark, all that is good, and all that is seeking marriage with the prince are very positive aspects of the feminine in her varying stages of growth.

The number *three*, a recurring theme in fairy tales, is another potent symbol of the feminine. Numerologically, three is associated with joy, happiness, communication, and creativity. It is the number of the trinity, the Triple Goddess. In classical geometry, the triangle or the trine is the mathematical expression of harmony, balance, and fluidity. The power of three unites the triangular flow of harmonic energies so that one may reach a pinnacle or state of higher consciousness, symbolized by the upright triangle. The downward pointing triangle represents the Yoni, or the feminine, which ushers one toward the dark, moist interior and thus toward initiation and transformation through birth in the world of form. Three is the primary number of the Major Arcana, an evolutionary step along the royal path of wisdom in the tarot, whereby one must incarnate into the natural world.

The Empress—Trump number III in *Inner Child Cards*—represents nature, fertility, birth, sexuality, and creativity. Ancient alchemical texts refer to an egg-shaped hermetic vessel, or cosmic womb, within which various processes of transmutation occur. We find similar associations with The Empress card. She is connected to Mother Goose and the story of the "Golden Egg." This story has its origins in ancient Egypt where the Empress took the form of Mother Hathor, incarnated as the Nile Goose who laid the golden egg of the Sun. The Nile Goose was also referred to as the creator of the world, because she produced the whole universe in a primordial world egg. Likewise, the Empress is known as the Queen of the World, who richly bestows all of her treasures upon the earth.

Fairy tales often include the creative force of the number *three* in the form of three spells, three curses, or three initiations. We find three wishes, three sisters, three brothers, and three tasks to succeed at before the maiden's hand is won. Often on the third day, or on the third wish, or on the third try, behind the third door, or after the third knock, something magical will happen. We have the three little pigs, the three bears, three cups, three bowls, and three chairs and beds. Fairy tales such as "The Three Feathers," "The Three Golden Hairs," "The Three Languages," and "The Three Little Men in the Woods" teach the importance of personal integrity and restraint concerning magic and wishing.

EACH CHARACTER IS A DIFFERENT ASPECT OF ONE'S OWN PSYCHE, SEEKING WHOLENESS THROUGH ALCHEMICAL MARRIAGE

Children tend to absorb all of the parts of the fairy tale into themselves without judgment, and at different stages of the story become all of its characters. The older we become, the less likely we are to approach fairy tales in this holistic and alchemical way. In the days of oral storytelling, a gifted storyteller could spellbind everyone into an understanding of the truest meaning of the tale. Unfortunately, the art of storytelling has largely been lost. Today, when we listen to a story, we usually understand it in only the most superficial terms. We can remedy this by going deeper into understanding the archetypes of the characters as representing aspects of ourselves.

The duality between the good mother and the bad mother lives within all of us. The dark queen represents the part of the psyche that hungers for love and affection. Because she has been so thoroughly and consistently denied, she has become distorted and taken on the appearance of evil. It is only by embracing her—in a kind of alchemical marriage between different aspects of the female psyche—that we discover her true beauty and become whole.

The saga of most tales also involves movement toward an al-chemical marriage of another sort, where the inner Sun, the mascu-line, and the inner Moon, the feminine, unite. This union enables the individual to "live happily ever after"—to be fully self-realized and awake. The father of the tales is often a merchant, representing the earthly realm, somewhat like The Emperor in the Major Arcana—Trump number IV. The four is fixed and squares itself, so we see more conflict in the archetype of The Emperor.

The Emperor without his Queen or Empress is lost and only half able to be in service, which is why he is shortsighted and unable to see the wicked things that the stepmother is doing to his daughter. He has lost touch with the anima, or the Eternal Queen's love, and can only provide the material means by which to support his child. This is why he goes away on trips and in several tales asks the daugh-ters what they would like him to bring home to them. He does just what he is told. He brings wealth and riches home to the earth-bound, selfish sisters, and odd, symbolic gifts—like a hazelnut branch or a black rose—for his dear child of the heavens. His job is to set the form and provide the foundation.

The most vital and important male archetype in a fairy tale is typically that of the prince. Ultimately, he represents the action will of the feminine. The prince must find his way to the female protago-nist and awaken her. He is Mars and the part of the human psyche that must merge with the feminine in order to operate fully and responsibly. When the prince wins the maiden, we embrace our po-tential for wholeness and balance. This alchemical marriage must take place within each of us before we can ever be fully awakened in the path of true relationship.

When Empress and Emperor meet, the union of opposites has occurred and we are staged to meet Trump number V. In traditional tarot, he is The Hierophant who merges the principles of spirit and matter, or church and state. In *Inner Child Cards*, the Wizard Gandalf from *The Lord of the Rings* represents this step of evolution. With his golden staff, he plays the role of spiritual guardian, dedicated to sustaining the goodness of the Fellowship and safeguarding the magic of the golden ring.

Ultimately, out of The Empress comes The Earth Child—Trump number XXI in *Inner Child Cards*—traditionally known as The World. This card is 21, and 2+1=3, the magic number of the divine Trinity and of the Holy Mother who bears the cosmic Earth Child, or Soul of the World, uniting the spiritual aspects of freedom and form with the earthly aspects of productivity and creativity. This Earth Child, born of The Empress, is the ultimate expression of awakened wholeness. Here we come full circle, from the motherless child who wanders the world lost and cut off from its heavenly mother, to The Earth Child, who has come home to rest in the womb of the Great Mother, even while being fully alive and awake in the world.

Chapter 2

Initiation, Enchantment, and Awakening

We all walk amid mysteries. We are surrounded by an atmosphere in which we do not know at all what is going on or how it is linked to our destinies. So much is certain, however, that under special circumstances the sensitive feelers of our souls can reach beyond the limits of the body, and the soul is granted a presentiment, indeed a real view of the future.

—Goethe

Our souls are always driving us to find the deeper meaning of our existence. Like the Zen koan that asks, "What was your Original Face before you were born?" and Snow White's evil stepmother's query as she gazes into the mirror, "Mirror, Mirror on the wall, who's the fairest of them all?" we are always aching to know who we truly are. We seek to discern the karmic imprints of our souls and to nurture those imprints into the creative expressions for which we are destined.

Fairy tales and myths provide us with many valuable clues and signposts on the journey to fulfilling our destinies. Symbolically, they represent unconscious content, while appealing to both unconscious and conscious levels of awareness. Ultimately, the purpose of the tale is to awaken one to a higher state of selfhood—a revelation, renewal, or rebirth toward a dynamic wholeness or alchemical marriage between the anima and animus, male and female aspects of the soul.

In the world of fairy tales, the search for truth invariably overshadows all other inquiries. A good deed is ultimately rewarded, and, in the end, the innocent of heart and mind prevail. The fairy tale is a mystical story, stemming from an oral folklore tradition that seeks to teach the higher virtues of life through simple stories and sagas. It is nothing short of an alchemical adventure where mortals and beasts, and the forces of dark and light, intermix. What is accomplished, finally, is the transmutation of human evil into goodness. This is not an easy task, for within the woven magic of the story lies the true test of the soul.

The fairy tale has the potential to awaken and enlighten its audience, guiding us toward a nobler path, by way of myriad earthly temptations. For example, stories such as "The Midas Touch" and "The Emperor's New Clothes" show us the tragic outcome of a life motivated by greed and characterized by the misuse of power. Characters such as the stepsisters in "Cinderella," the wicked stepmother in "Snow White," and the uninvited thirteenth fairy in "Sleeping Beauty" vividly demonstrate the truism that a selfish, jealous heart can only lead to misery and loneliness.

In contrast to characters like these who represent the folly of human evil, we find protagonists such as Cinderella, Snow White, and Beauty (in "Beauty and the Beast") who offer a glimpse into the humble soul of goodness. Through such characters, we learn that those who endure hardship and suffering with a pure, open heart will, in the end, fulfill their destinies and live happily ever after.

Fairy tales offer simple truths. Yet, within their simple narrative structure, we are inspired to examine our own path to destiny and truth, for it must be remembered that the fairy tale seeks to awaken the soul to rise up, like a shining star, to its highest destiny. Because they reveal and expose hidden aspects of the unconscious, fairy tales also challenge us to examine the weak and frail aspects of the self that would lead one to tell a lie like Pinocchio, open the forbidden door as in "The Fairy Queen and the Wood Cutter's Child," or disobey and veer off the beaten path like Little Red Cap. To the extent these human weaknesses are uncovered, they can be healed.

As one's weaknesses are identified and healed, psychic space becomes available for the discovery and cultivation of previously hidden virtues and dormant strengths. These are typically brought to light in fairy tales by immortal creatures—angels, fairies, magical beasts, mermaids, enchanted birds or fish—or by beings such as talking trees or flowers, wishing wells, the moon, and the stars. These are the muses in the story who deliver rhyme, riddle, and message; they cast spells and curses, bless and redeem, frightening and curing us at the same time.

As we examine the therapeutic landscape in the magical world of fairy tales, certain predictable patterns or stages of transformation become evident. First, there is an initiation through hardship and difficulty. Next comes a time of enchantment that lightens the heart and guides the weary seeker along the path. Finally, the protagonist is awakened to his or her soul's destiny.

We find instructive parallels in ancient alchemical texts, which speak of the process of transmutation occurring in stages referred to as: 1) Melanosis (blackening) 2) Leukosis (whitening) 3) Xanthosis (yellowing) and 4) Iosis (reddening). Several centuries ago, these colors were reduced to three—black, white, and red—with the color yellow being subsumed within the color red. These remaining colors correspond to the fairy tale stages of: 1) initiation, 2) enchantment, and 3) awakening, respectively.

INITIATION: CORRESPONDING TO
THE ALCHEMICAL STAGE OF MELANOSIS

As the soul incarnates and moves through its progressive stages—birth, identity of self, transformation, death, and rebirth—it undergoes various initiations that are experienced as tests. In the quest for life's mastery, we find that the individual must meet certain challenges that will help him or her to excel. These challenges invariably occur in karmically appropriate ways in order to offer the lessons best suited to the particular individual.

The search for meaning and purpose pulls the individual toward soulful solutions to life's challenges and the ultimate fulfillment of his or her destiny. Legends, myths, stories, and fables all assist one in answering the eternal questions: "What is the world really like?" "How am I to live my life in it?" "How can I truly be myself?" Each of us, at whatever age—for we circle around and meet this initiation again and again in one lifetime—must find images and symbols that conform to our deepest convictions and interior complexities. Only then can we embrace renewed and awakened motifs of our future selves. Most importantly on this journey of awakening, one must find a way to enter the void of the unconscious where darkened, divine waters hold the wisdom of past, present, and future.

In fairy tales, the time of initiation takes various forms. One wanders lost through a dark forest, or encounters a Dark Mother, a wicked witch, a frightful beast, or a dragon. This is a time when the umbilical cord is cut from the nurturing force of the golden rays of protection and the protagonist must find his or her own way—Snow White is lost in the woods; Rapunzel is locked in the Tower; Beauty goes off to the Beast's castle, into the unknown territory that holds the key to her destiny. Fairy-tale heroes or heroines must do the work of their own soul—through the suffering they endure and the ways they experience and find meaning in the midst of hardship. The tears of their sorrows often water and moisten the potential for future growth.

The blackness of this initiatory stage represents the beginning, the fertilization and gestation of creative potential, the prima materia or chaos out of which the elements are born. Fairy-tale myth brings us to a darkened part of ourselves, our suffering, as well as to our quest for a greater life. This quest propels us toward inevitable polarity, out of darkness toward the light. We aim our longing toward our other half where we seek the union of the male and female, known in alchemy as matrimonium, coitus, and coniunctio.

ENCHANTMENT: CORRESPONDING TO THE ALCHEMICAL STAGE OF LEUKOSIS

In the magical landscape of the fairy tale, this stage is typically symbolized by a white dove, fallen snow, a wedding dress, or lilies and roses. At this stage, mystical creatures, happenings, and miracles often act as mediators within the context of the story. After one has wandered in the darkness, so to speak, one comes to a place, meets a person, talks to a frog, touches the spindle, or finds a magic helper of some sort. This is the enchantment or the alchemical whitening stage. At this point, the curse or the spell will be released and the human being becomes engaged with purification and moving toward renewal and rebirth.

Enchantment is part of the process of awakening. We may see glimpses of the gold or the truth, and we know we are heading in that direction, but the final act of redemption, freedom, or revelation has not happened. After having been lost in the woods and imprisoned in the candy house, Hansel and Gretel realize they are not in a fantasyland. Through the work of their own inner will, they free themselves from the curse or spell that came to them from the darkened part of their human journey. Before finding their own true riches they were cared for by a stepmother who had little love for them (their own lost self-love), and so they needed to find a way to resurrect and find unconditional love.

In "Sleeping Beauty," enchantment, or whitening, occurs at the moment Sleeping Beauty awakens from 100 years of sleep. In the tale of "Rapunzel," a moment of enchantment occurs when Rapunzel's long, beautiful braids, representing her ego identity, are sheared by the enchantress, freeing her to extricate herself from the curse of captivation and solitude. Banished to a desert, Rapunzel must now nourish the darkened, fertile aspects of her own real life force by doing the work of her soul. In this way, she offers the elixir of her suffering, her tears, to the fates that lie before her.

This process of enchantment is followed by the death of the individual ego, which merges into the white, also referred to as the washing or baptisma in alchemy. Here the soul and matter become one and the process toward greater understanding is attained. One moves toward the goal. In many fables we find that a winter snow has fallen, symbolizing a stage of stillness and quiet, a time of inner reflection before the awakening will occur.

AWAKENING: CORRESPONDING TO THE ALCHEMICAL STAGES OF XANTHOSIS AND IOSIS

The yellowing aspect of awakening is typically symbolized in fairy tales by the golden castle, the chalice, the apple, the key, and coins. These symbols represent that part of us that seeks the ideal, the manifestation of the awakened self, or the jewel of the heart. Though we begin our journey in a time of initiation or darkness, this, of course, is merely the human aspect of our birth. We are, in fact, of golden origins, hence the hidden gold that must be found.

The reddening aspect of awakening is often symbolized in fairy-tale lore by the passionate sunrise of a new day, fire, or the dragon's fiery breath. These images of heat heighten the intensity of transformation. A profound state of wholeness is achieved as all delusions and mistaken notions of self are burned away in the fire of pure awareness. Regarding mistaken or incomplete notions of self, we must not forget that all characters within a fable are aspects of the nonintegrated human being. At different stages of life we come into contact with these various parts of ourselves. The goal is to integrate into a wholeness that synthesizes these lesser parts into the one greater whole where mind, heart, body, and soul function in harmony.

Through the process of awakening, we learn that the material and the spiritual aspects of life are equally valuable. What we perceive as material reality is only one-half of the whole; the content of the human spirit is the other half. The fairy tale lifts the veil to nature, the soul of humanity, and the creation of the world. Each enchantment breaks a spell and leads us ever closer to the picture of the finished world—the world of perfection and purity that lives within the heart of the individual. In the words of Goethe:

> When the healthy nature of man works as one whole, when he feels himself to exist in the world as in a great and beautiful whole, when the harmonious sense of well-being imparts to him a pure, free delight, the Universe—if it could be conscious of itself—having attained its goal, would shout for joy and admire the summit of its own becoming and being.*

*I found this quote from Goethe in a book by the German theosophist Rudolf Steiner— Rudolf Steiner, *The Essential Steiner* (New York: HarperCollins, 1984), 22.

Chapter 3

The Archetypes of the Soul and Karmic Imprints

The reality accessible to mere perception is only the one-half of the whole reality; the content of the human spirit is the other half. . . . Man is not only there in order to form for himself a picture of the finished world; nay, he himself cooperates in bringing the world into existence.

—Rudolf Steiner,
The Essential Steiner

The wisdom of the soul is found in the intricate design of human mythology and the stories of creation. The root of our theological, psychological, intellectual, and creative history is buried in an ancient heritage layered with diverse civilizations and symbols. Traces of legend, song, myth, architecture, icon, and language lend mystery to our imagination, which, in turn, produces a future framed with virtues of the past and the inventions of time. This ancient timelessness ripens a potential within the individual that is as profound as it is ordinary, for we are a complex blend of temporal, spiritual, and invisible forces.

The desire to understand our own multi-faceted stories compels us to search for fragments of unknown and unseen aspects of culture, as well as the imprints they mark upon us. As we embark upon this enchanted search, we dream of ideals yet to be realized, and, simultaneously, gaze upon the real stuff of everyday life. The creative stories of the soul live between the cracks of heavenly and earthly realms. In the depths of our longing for greater meaning, we find ourselves poised between cultures of immeasurable beauty and those of great misery and strife.

Our reaching toward meaning constitutes a human drive to actualize the bounty of a destiny fulfilled. When it is denied, we are woefully disconnected from the lifeline of the soul. As we attempt to revive the body of wisdom from the skeleton of antiquity, we find extraordinary evidence of genius progressing from one civilization to the next. The archaeology of the soul is a treasure to be seized and reclaimed again and again. Nature, myth, and the stories of time offer humanity fuel for inevitable change and new growth, the only aspect of life that is undeniably predictable.

Each recovered truth adds to the fabric of a sacred garment whose outer edges extend into the folds of the collective imagination, allowing us to retrieve the well-worn stories of our ancient, hidden past, reweaving them and pulling them upward toward the light. Casting these passages of wisdom into the light of a conscious mind allows fertile seeds of imagination to germinate. In daily life it becomes the task of the individual to awaken this mythology and reach high and wide toward the discovery of self.

FAIRY TALES: LIBERATORS OF THE SOUL

Deemed mere childhood fantasies, the true meanings of fairy tales have often been veiled and hidden, but the teachings of the soul are revealed in these stories we have come to know and love. For centuries, fairy tales have been an oral dialogue between mortal humans and the enchanted configurations of nature, the animal kingdom, fairies, angels, and all that the imagination can produce. Fairy stories serve as a stepping-stone between worlds, offering humanity a magical tour into our unending search for wholeness. The treasure trove of mythological texts surviving from our ancestral past confirms that our deepest quest for love and truth is a recurring theme at the heart of the fairy tale. Historically, these stories have been passed down from generation to generation, creating the backbone of human ethics and values. The genius of a well-worn story is revealed by its longevity and survival through the ages and its ability to restore hope and faith in humanity's search for love.

Stories may enter the gates of the mind when an individual has unlocked the forbidden latch to imagination and freedom. Once this internal oppression is removed from the psyche, the seeker is ready to journey into the awakened terrain of the higher mind. Endowed with innocence and fresh perspectives, the individual discovers ways he or she may liberate the metaphorical ghosts, dragons, beasts, and wicked aspects of the mind, for the fairy tale awakens the unconscious. When the unconscious is brought to light, one transcends the barriers of fear and limitation, and, with constant striving, attains freedom.

Fairy tales invoke within the soul a need to arise and meet one's truest self, to gain integrity, and to live a pure and simple life, one that honors the authentic beauty within nature and humanity. Instead of living blindly from moment to moment, our hope is to live in true awareness and consciousness as we move toward a fulfilled future. Those who prosper in wealth of spirit have found meaning and purpose in their lives. They serve the world with a fierce commitment to fulfil their highest destinies. The process by which such a destiny is fulfilled involves ever-widening and deepening spheres of karmic and archetypal influence being brought to bear upon each of us in myriad ways.

In Chapter One, we examined the notion that each character in a fairy tale represents an aspect of one's own psyche yearning for integration or alchemical marriage with its other parts. We also considered the idea that all the characters in a fairy tale—even those that appear evil—are ultimately good. As already noted, this is because fairy tales are intrinsically soulful and feminine. Whether they nurture us in gentle ways, or are challengingly fierce, they are essentially compassionate catalysts for growth.

In Chapter Two, we explored the three stages of growth that typically occur within the context of fairy-tale lore: initiation, enchantment, and awakening. The fairy-tale protagonist initially wanders around in shadowy places, lost and orphaned, cut off from his or her true spiritual identity and home. At some point in the narrative—after much suffering in this dark night of the soul—the protagonist receives a blessing or magical enchantment of some sort. This boon offers a glimpse of the spiritual light at the end of the tunnel, so to speak. Finally, through the process of enduring great hardship and overcoming many obstacles, the hero or heroine emerges victorious, awakening to his or her true, golden self and the unfolding of destiny.

KARMIC IMPRINTS

With these foundation stones in mind, we turn to the topic of karmic imprints and the archetypes of the individual soul. Karma is a very complex thing, much more subtle and intricate than we have been led to believe. In its most basic form, karma is a spiritual law of cause and effect—similar to the ancient notion of "as you sow, shall you reap." Every action an individual takes has repercussions—for his or herself, for loved ones, and for the world—not only in one life, but for future incarnations as well. Karmic imprints are the memories or carried-over effects of past lifetimes, positive or negative, that are stored within the unconscious banks of the human body, mind, and soul.

Our task as human beings is to liberate and free ourselves from any limiting residue of the past that may be blocking our ability to thrive in this lifetime. A tremendous amount of study and research continues as humanity explores the depth and complexity of this issue. Methods such as past-life regression work, rebirthing, hypnotic therapy, and several modalities of bodywork assist one toward the discovery of these past blocks and emotional trigger points.

Each of us has our own unique karmic situation, which affects how we proceed through the various stages on the path to eventual awakening. Among other things, our karmic imprints, or soul prints, help determine which archetypal energies we will find most compelling and transformative. For instance, if a soul in previous incarnations has had traumatic experiences in the realm of personal empowerment and authority (perhaps that soul was imprisoned for daring to express views honestly in a situation where those in power wanted to hide that particular truth) then that person may have a problem with expression in this lifetime. Such individuals may stutter, hold back communications with others in fear of condemnation, or feel as though they are not heard or affirmed in life. The ability to bring this unconscious pattern into conscious understanding allows the individual to liberate from the confines of this particular limitation. Often, the process involves tremendous trust, faith, and willingness to tackle this internal issue. However, successfully healed, the individual will find new freedom and joy in this lifetime.

To begin to understand one's own set of karmic conditions, it's important to consider the many spheres of karmic patterning that overlap and interweave in any given life. Collective dimensions of karma—such as national, socio-economic, racial, and gender identities—play a major role in the unfolding of one's life and destiny, yet these obvious conditioning factors often go unacknowledged or are not given the attention they deserve.

Each culture and civilization has its own paradigms and rituals, its own overriding mythology, and its own collective karma or group consciousness—all of which shape the bigger picture within which each individual approaches his or her destiny. It is important to keep this in mind as we set out on life's great odyssey. In a complex world where puzzle pieces are more easily discernable than the big picture, it behooves us to retrieve and understand both our personal and collective mythologies. These will serve as valuable road maps and mile markers along the way. Fables of yesteryear shine a light into the soulful inner caverns of humanity, and on the mighty struggle between the forces of good and evil being waged therein.

As a citizen of the United States, the wealthiest and most powerful nation in the world, I've found myself reflecting upon fairy-tale mythology as it relates to the potential hazards of such material abundance and power. Several relevant stories come to mind, most significantly J. R. R. Tolkien's masterful tale *The Lord of the Rings*, which revolves around the heroic adventures of the young hobbit, Frodo Baggins. Frodo, in his innocence and goodness, has been given the daunting task of saving Middle Earth from the devastating, seductive influence of the will to absolute domination, symbolized by a golden ring. In order to negate the evil power of the ring, the little hobbit must return it to the place where it was created—the fiery core of the volcano of Mount Doom.

Along the way, Frodo experiences great hardship and many life-threatening dangers. He is protected and assisted by various elves, humans, hobbits, and dwarves, each of whom eventually succumbs to the dangerous lure of the ring. Frodo himself is not entirely immune to the ring's power. In fact, the longer he is in possession of it and the closer his proximity to it, the more difficult his task becomes. Finally, at the close of the epic tale, Frodo stands poised at the edge of the pool of molten lava in the cavernous bowels of Mount Doom. There he struggles mightily with himself, but finds that he has lost the will to renounce the ring and its will to dominate. He cannot summon the inner strength to remove the ring from his finger and cast it into the fire from which it was forged. Indeed, it is only by a fortuitous accident that the ring is torn from his finger and dissolved back into the great womb of the Earth.

The ring in *The Lord of the Rings* is a potent symbol of the dangers to the spirit that are part and parcel of life in the wealthiest and most powerful nation in the world. Remembering that power corrupts and absolute power corrupts absolutely, I find myself pondering the extent to which my beloved country has been corrupted by its most privileged position vis-à-vis the rest of the world. To what extent have we been blinded and spiritually compromised by our wealth and power; to what extent am I personally implicated in all of this? In general, I wonder about the karmic consequences for the individual of the misuse of wealth and power on a national scale. These are painful but important questions that can motivate us to act compassionately and responsibly in the world. As we venture down the path of self-awakening, toward the land of "happily ever after," we are reminded by *The Lord of the Rings* that evil can only be healed of its devastating power through dissolution back into the source.

When the soul of humanity has been starved and exhausted by long, aimless wandering, a universal hunger prevails. Such hunger can be misdirected into overconsumption of the world's precious resources. In fairy tales, we are often presented with a story line where a character confuses the false food of self-gratification with the real food of soul-gratification. For example, the stepsisters in "Cinderella" seek the pleasures of the material world and adorn themselves with its riches, while remaining painfully unaware of the true riches of the soul. They have been imprinted with the wound of their biological mother—a jealous, vain, greedy, and selfish person representing the shadow side of love. Unlike Cinderella, they have not been released from the umbilical of the mother; they have not been orphaned into the initiation of selfhood. Thus they are not ready to move toward sacrifice or self-awakening.

Cinderella's stepsisters represent the part of humanity that is blind to the subtle and sublime aspects of compassion and care. In the end of Grimm's traditional version of the story, they are literally blinded, symbolizing the fate that comes to one who is unable to see beyond the realm of self-indulgence. In the words of the ancient text:

> Suddenly the doves, who were still sitting on Cinderella's shoulder, picked an eye out of each, and as the sisters came from the church, they picked out the other eye. So, as a deserved punishment for their wickedness and deception, they were smitten with blindness during the rest of their lives.*

In the story of Cinderella, the two white doves that poke out the eyes of the stepsisters had helped Cinderella with the impossible tasks she had been given each day. They perched upon a tree that grew from the twig of a hazelnut branch given to Cinderella by her father on his return from a voyage. Cinderella had planted the twig on her mother's grave and wept upon the site three times each day. A great tree grew from her tears. It held within its branches the birds that protected Cinderella and granted her wishes. Through her tears, Cinderella merged with the spirit world (the doves) and nature (the Tree of Life). They opened the doors to her everlasting union with her whole self—physical, emotional, mental, and spiritual. Cinderella's suffering brought forward her compassion and willingness to be of service, attributes found amongst the men and women of the world who aim for soul expression, filling the world with grace by the example of their word and deed.

Grimm's Fairy Tales (New York: McLaughlin Bros., 1891), 111.

FAIRY-TALE SYMBOLISM REPLENISHES THE SOUL

In the great fairy story of life, we can open to new characters and endings if we wish, but the basic themes must remain integral if we are to glean wisdom from the ages. Humanity craves something constant—a food that nourishes both the spiritual and mundane components of life. Fairy tales, through the ages, have been ladled from a pot of symbolism that replenishes the soul with the stuff of goodness, justice, and everlasting enchantment. A story that teaches global truths and morality will stand the test of time and be retold over and over again. The characters and symbols of a fable change as each culture molds the imagery of the story into the framework of an existing social network, making restoration of the original text almost impossible. However, the general theme and moral of a beloved tale survives the ages.

Let us examine the fable of "Jack and the Beanstalk." The universal truths of this fable extend beyond earthly limitations, for the umbilical that connects the heaven and the earth is the very stalk that Jack climbs in order to gain the riches of his soul. The myth of Jack and the Beanstalk can be traced back into African folklore. The stalk was originally that of the fava bean tree, a tree that houses the beasts of the jungle, particularly the giant ape. When the ape grapples to free himself from the entanglements of the bristling branches, a shower of fava beans covers the earth. The fall of the ape out of the tree becomes, in essence, the giant's fall from the sky that liberated Jack and his mother, allowing them to attain their heavenly treasures.

In many fairy tales a baby born to royalty is blessed with the virtues of beauty and riches. However, as fate will have it, the child meets with unexpected poverty, cruelty, sacrifice, and injustice. The character's plunge into the midst of a mortal struggle clutches at the heart of our own life story, for we must encounter the boundaries of heaven and engage with prima materia, the substance of earth. The tragic fall from the proverbial Tree of Life marks the fateful beginning of the fool's journey—the inexplicable encounter with the abyss of infinite potential. At this juncture, the individual meets the complexities of light and dark that color the passages of life's initiation. We are all at the mercy of a fateful journey, and what better way could there be to understand the vagaries of life than through the lens of a fairy tale, where the profound mystery of the soul is revealed through the eyes of a child.

In our everyday language we have all heard the phrases: "the kiss of fate," "the kiss of death," and "sealed with a kiss." The intimate action of a kiss has been portrayed, through the ages, as something magical and enchanting. A kiss has various meanings; however, there is a meeting place where all kisses intersect, a place where the deepest imprint of a kiss is forever planted within the heart. It is romantic, healing, assuring, and affirming. The everlasting sweetness of a kiss is exchanged when, and only when, the kiss has been offered with the greatest of intention and kindness. When a child falls and bruises a knee, it is not the kiss that heals the tender wound, but the intention and care the kiss portrays. This kiss of kindness transforms the experience of hurting into one of magic, for suddenly, without rational reasoning, the bump feels better. This precious moment lingers within the soul and touches the edges of heavenly protection, for it is love, and love alone, that invites the divine presence of healing.

In fairy-tale lore, the kiss is offered as a potent metaphor. For example, various tales include a kiss at the epic moment when the wheel of fate turns toward revival, happiness, awakening, and transformation. A kiss is an act of will; it is a deliberate action that denotes a desire to communicate in a nonverbal fashion. Therefore, a kiss carries breath and life force to the other. In the tale of Snow White, when the third curse of the wicked enchantress—the bite of the poison apple—is lodged within the throat of Snow White, it is the kiss of the prince that restores her breath. The dwarves are unable to assist her, for it must be the work of her own soul that will bring her back to life. Her potential to initiate and awaken into freedom and service has arrived. The prince—her active and masculine psyche— represents her own will to live and love, despite the pain and suffering visited upon her by her wicked stepmother, representing part of her unconscious shadow and darkness. The beautiful princess—symbol of the beautiful soul of each individual—must engage with various stages of initiation and enchantment before entering the golden castle of self-actualization.

The fairy tale seeks to open a door so that we may cross its threshold into wholeness and love. I often call this door the Crystal Door. It holds within its framework the rainbow spectrum of possibilities each of us must meet if we are to hold true to our highest dreams and allow the light of love and wisdom to be our entryway into a new life. Until we have found the rightful key to the Crystal Door of our own joy, we may not fully extend our heart outward in service. This is the plight of the initiate. In the quest for awakening, one will invariably stumble into the many lessons and teachings life has to offer. However, when one fully engages with the multi-dimensional aspects of nature, humanity, and the invisible or hidden worlds, one comes to realize how precious is life and how profound the need to balance body and soul.

Fairy tales nourish the stale and hardened constructs of the mind by bringing moisture to the landscape of life through innocent and perceptive virtues. They offer the same medicine as psychoanalysis in many ways, for both afford a process by which individuals may move through and come to understand the suffering, trauma, challenges, and changes in life without being defeated by them.

For example, many fairy tales begin with the death of a mother or father, and this crushing blow at a young age profoundly and dramatically alters the life of the child. The fairy-tale heroine or hero has been orphaned and cut off from the nourishment and umbilical safety and security of the matrix of life, or Manna, the Great Mother. This theme becomes the defining metaphor for all living beings. We must all let go of the umbilical cord of the Cosmic Mother, our spiritual origins, in order to become flesh and blood and fully human, so that we may continue to evolve and aspire toward our destiny.

This is the plight of Pinocchio. As he travels through the trials and tribulations of his life, his little wooden body careens toward the consequences of his lies. When he turns into a donkey with big donkey ears, representing his need to listen and pay attention to his conscience, we witness an example of the outcome of folly and deception. Eventually, Pinocchio approaches the summit of his initiation in life: he learns that the truth will set him free from his misery and, consequently, becomes a real little boy. He is able to join his maker Gepetto, a man with a warm and kind heart who loves him unconditionally. Gepetto is, of course, symbolic of our own maker or spiritual source. We, like Pinocchio, must find our way through life's challenges until we find our way back home—back to our whole and intact creative selves.

Fairy tales illuminate various archetypal dilemmas so that we may examine the complexities of the plot of life. They are made simple so that the heart can see beyond the opposition of good and evil, for example. Characters are wholly wicked, clever, deceitful, innocent, good, or earnest in order to magnify the basic duality that poses such a challenge in our lives. The polarization and conflict within the tale enables us to explore truths and virtues without having to create a complex theory or bias about the outcome of the situation. In his book *The Uses of Enchantment*, Bruno Bettelheim writes:

The more simple and straightforward a good character, the easier it is for a child to identify with it and to reject the bad other. The child identifies with the good hero not because of his goodness, but because the hero's condition makes a deep positive appeal to him. The question for the child is not "Do I want to be good?" but "Who do I want to be like?" The child decides this on the basis of projecting himself wholeheartedly into one character.*

In its highest form, this character becomes an aspect of the inner world of the child and helps to form the framework of a sturdy and well-adjusted identity. Projecting ourselves into fairy-tale characters and identifying with them wholeheartedly can help us understand who we are and why we are here. It can assist in the difficult task of reading our soul maps, in discerning the faint patterns of our unique karmic imprints, so that we may fully express our deepest and best selves in the world of form.

*Bruno Bettelheim, *The Uses of Enchantment* (New York: Vintage Books, 1975), 10.

Chapter 4

Fairy-Tale Mysticism and the Major Arcana

Throughout the creation of the *Inner Child Cards*—a revolutionary set of the ancient tarot—one profound idea played a dominant role. The selected fairy-tale stories and key images fit the twenty-two Trumps of the Major Arcana in an astounding way. The magical fairy tales told the wisdom of the Royal Road of the tarot even better than the usual pictures of Fool, Magician, High Priestess, Empress, and so on. We found ourselves wondering why this was happening. What had we discovered by relating fairy tales to the Major Trumps?

TAROT AND FAIRY TALES: BRANCHES ON THE TREE OF ANCIENT KNOWLEDGE

The best answer is that both the tarot and fairy-tale mysticism are branches of the universal teachings of ageless wisdom. More profoundly, these branches are located on the same tree of ancient knowledge—a knowledge lost in the dim recesses of civilizations that flourished eons ago, but were then snuffed out by a global flood, an inundation that destroyed much of humanity.

Even a cursory study of the twenty-two Major Arcana for *Inner Child Cards* will reveal connections between fairy tales and Trumps that amaze the mind. For instance, the profound links associating "Aladdin and the Magic Lamp" with The Magician, "Snow White and the Seven Dwarves" with The Hermit, "Rapunzel" with The Tower, and "Cinderella" with The Moon are too precise to ignore. We might say that when these fairy tales were originally created— probably more as oral traditions that were passed down through the ages, eventually becoming written and then printed stories—they locked into the archetypes of the Major Arcana of the tarot that were existing within the collective consciousness of humanity. This brings us to the wisdom contained within the works of Carl Jung, Joseph Campbell, and other writer/psychologists of the modern era.

The human species is surrounded or even immersed in a kind of etheric web of enlightened wisdom. This wisdom is an emanation of divine intelligences that human beings know little about, although the great philosophers, sages, and prophets of the past have tried to stammer out an understanding of this universal language. As each individual is born and evolves within a particular language, culture, and society, he or she opens up to the potential of tapping into the secrets of the collective unconscious of the human race. Mythology itself—or the myth-making capacity of the human mind—is a province of the collective unconscious. Thus, it is global in scope, relating to all nations, continents, and civilizations, present or past. Both fairy-tale mysticism and the tarot, as a system of ancient knowledge, exist somewhere within the realm of mythology and humanity's vast unconscious network of ideas, thoughts, images, and stories. When the Grimm Brothers were searching for the puzzle pieces to the stories of our past, they said it was like finding fragments of a mirror.

Each of you reading this workbook can access this web of wisdom; you have the capacity to discover your own deep connections to fairy tales and their links to the tarot. Through dreams, flashes of insight, meditations, affirmations, and waking visions, you can weave new threads together in the illustrious garment of the tarot that has been evolving through the ages. For instance, in light of what has already been shared in the previous book and the three preceding chapters in this companion guide, ponder the following: *The Major Arcana of the tarot can be considered a fairy tale!* No one knows the true origin of these cards of universal wisdom. Just as fairy tales were a part of oral traditions, handed down through the generations and eventually finding their way into the printed word, the Major Arcana were an oral tradition of pictorial knowledge—a system, language, or tool for accessing divine wisdom. We do know that modern tarot cards suddenly appeared in France in the late 1300s. Before that, the trail is rather murky, with many extraordinary legends about the origins of the cards, involving ancient Egypt, the wandering gypsies, and European knights traveling through the Middle East and bringing back unusual teachings. However, based on many of the myths regarding the origin of the Major Trumps, one can put together the following fairy tale.

> Once upon a time, there was a great civilization known as Atlantis. This land existed on several islands in what is now known as the Atlantic Ocean. Over millennia, the people of this realm developed incredible arts, sciences, and educational centers. The Atlanteans were closer to the divine and magical worlds than we are today. Just as we have television and radio, many of the advanced members of that race had developed clairvoyance and clairaudience. Psychic powers and picking up on other people's thoughts and feelings were the norm—not rare occurrences. The astral realm of dreams was much more real to the Atlanteans than it is in our own era. These people thought more in pictures, images, and stories than we do. One of the greatest discoveries in Atlantis was that of the Major Arcana of the tarot—along with the original fairy-tale stories associated with the cards—as a system for staying in touch with divine wisdom. People didn't go

to card readers to have their fortunes told; they lived the tarot in their waking lives, relationships, families, adventures, and professions. However, while Atlantis was filled with many marvels of ancient technology, architecture, and artistic brilliance, there was a dark side of the culture. The power to harness the rays of the sun was developed and transformed into a crystal of enormous power. Although it was originally intended as a protective device to provide light, sustenance, and radiance to the Atlantean civilization, negative figures within the governmental hierarchy conspired to use the crystal against adversary nations. Just as our current world grapples with the power of nuclear energy, the ancient Atlanteans began fearing that the crystal might become their downfall. Sensing a looming disaster, the intuitive priests and priestesses of Atlantis put the complete package of arcane symbolism, teachings, and wisdom of their land together in the twenty-two Major Trumps of the tarot. They knew they couldn't save their homes, possessions, and even many of their loved ones, but they could preserve an understanding of the ageless wisdom that would somehow live on even if Atlantis perished. Lo and behold, the crystal was used in a destructive fashion and Atlantis was rocked by volcanic eruptions and tsunami floods. However, the keepers of the secret teachings concealed within the tarot escaped in the nick of time to Egypt, where their knowledge helped to create a new and mighty civilization, eventually symbolized by the mysterious Sphinx and the Great Pyramid. Even the Hebrew alphabet, with its twenty-two letters (based on pictures), sprang forth from the original twenty-two Major Arcana cards. And the English alphabet we use today is a direct descendant of the magic and wisdom hidden within the imaginatively alive Hebrew letters.

Is the fairy tale just presented based on truth? Probably. We will never know for sure, but many students of esoteric thought believe this is actually how the tarot was preserved and passed down through the ages. Some French scholars, like P. Christian and Edouard

Schure—as reported by Manly Palmer Hall in his magnum opus *The Secret Teachings of All Ages*—are strong proponents of the idea that a secret passageway once existed between the Sphinx and the Great Pyramid. Along this passageway, neophytes would walk on their way to their spiritual initiation within the Great Pyramid itself. While modern historians hold to the thought that this incredible structure was simply a burial place for the Pharaoh Cheops, those steeped in esoteric lore feel the Great Pyramid was much more than a mere tomb. It is possible that along the underground route between the Sphinx and the Great Pyramid were two rows of the twenty-two Major Trumps of the tarot, existing as a kind of higher-level awakening device for the person about to be initiated into an exalted order of wisdom. However, it is important to remember that the Major cards are cyclical in nature rather than linear.

THE MAJOR ARCANA: A CYCLICAL JOURNEY OF TRANSFORMATION

The traditional Major Arcana have a starting point (The Fool) and conclusion (The World), which should really be understood as a circle of evolution—not as a straight line! Similarly, the *Inner Child Cards* have a beginning of the archetypal story (Little Red Cap) and a satisfying end (The Earth Child). As described in *Inner Child Cards: A Fairy-Tale Tarot*, there is a wholeness, a total evolution at work in which Little Red Cap (the innocent Fool in search of universal wisdom) moves through each fairy-tale story and archetypal image within the *Inner Child Cards* journey. Eventually, Little Red Cap—through life, death, and the invisible realms of existence—transforms herself into The Earth Child, ready to incarnate once again on Spaceship Earth, and begin a new round of life as Little Red Cap again, on a higher turn of the spiral.

Throughout the *Inner Child Cards* Major Trumps, there is a mysterious pattern at work. Each fairy tale holds all the components of a whole story, with a beginning, middle, and end. Within the context of the story, stages of growth and initiation lead the main character(s) toward a better life, greater truth, personal wisdom, self-empowerment, and the miracle of rebirth that in fairy tales is called enchantment. There are stages of dark searching that must take place or deep sorrow and sadness that must be met in order for the soul to fully comprehend the impact of the experience as life-giving and sacred.

In the fairy tale, all of the characters symbolize parts of a whole human being. At different stages of our lives we may relate to different aspects of the tale. Children are very innocent and open; they very clearly see this distinction of character development. One day they might be the white horse, another day the princess, another day the wicked witch. The stories bring light to the soul within a greater context of society and the world-at-large, which is why the fairy tale can cross the boundaries of culture and race. We can all relate to the good deeds and the highest goals of success and goodwill. In fairy tales, we learn that the highest reward goes to those who have successfully met their inner dragon, faced it with true courage and conviction, and moved farther along the road to enlightenment.

Like each individual fairy tale, the Major Arcana has a beginning, middle, and end. However, the wanderer or seeker can begin at different stages at different times. The beauty of the tarot is that one can choose to study an archetype at any stage of life development and proceed from that particular place. Little Red Cap (The Fool) is the main jumping-off point because it stands at the beginning and end of the Major Trumps. In the traditional decks The Fool is literally seen at the edge of a cliff, ready and willing to take the leap into the unknown future. We might consider this card to be in an orphaned state, for the figure is alone with humble sack on back, headed for new experience, not attached to or secured by the past. A fairy story often begins with an orphaned child, born from a royal queen who dies at the start of the tale. The child must be cut from the umbilical of the golden cord that brought it to earth and find the road to individuation in spite of suffering and toil. Thus, the orphan child is a clear representation of The Fool, for inherent within the orphan's soul is the genius and inward cleverness to find its way to freedom and love. The Fool is also known as the jester or trickster who, without arrogance or stuffy intelligence, is able to move with candor and agility, finding a way to the greatest treasure. The reason this is possible is that The Fool is unattached to the imprints of the past. The Fool finds a new life, a new beginning, a new way to the riches of the spirit.

In many ways, *Inner Child Cards* Trump XIX, The Yellow Brick Road, is a kind of metaphor for the Major cards themselves. In traditional decks, a smiling child is seen, either riding a horse or dancing in a garden of sunflowers. This child is once again Little Red Cap, The Fool, or the orphaned child, now connected back to the Yellow Brick Road of the soul. Thus, the Major Arcana is an inspiring road map to higher levels of consciousness, the golden road to enlightenment. All of the Major cards and their fairy-tale counterparts are treasure-troves that reflect back to us aspects of our divinity.

Chapter 5

Mirrors to Humanity

One of life's great mysteries is that you can never see yourself as you really are. Think about it. You can only look out from your internal vantage point; seeing yourself as you truly are is *not* usually possible. However, with the help of the magical device known as the mirror, each of us becomes acquainted with an external reflection of our face, body, and form in the material world. We grow up seeing an evolution of our appearance—from childhood to maturity and old age—and we become attached to this image of ourselves. Like the vain and jealous stepmother-queen in the tale of Snow White who keeps gazing into her magic mirror looking for perfection, or the tragic mythological Greek figure of Narcissus who gazed adoringly at himself in a pond, most of us become entranced by and fall in love with (or become frustrated by) our own reflections. In one sense, this may seem to be the highest we can hope for—to understand ourselves from the outside in, through our reflections rather than our core reality. Nevertheless, there is a way of using the mirrors of life as tools that enable us to live more from the inside out, from our spiritual source, our highest divinity.

Mirrors are all around us, from the cosmic to the personal. Within the *Inner Child Cards*, the different types of cards—Trumps, court cards, and numbered cards—function as mirrors in different ways.

The eye is akin to a camera. And scientists tell us that the human eye—really an extension of the human brain and mind—has an in-built capacity to reverse images. As infants, we actually have to learn how to perceive the outside world correctly—otherwise everything might appear upside down!

THE TRUMPS: THE SOUL'S JOURNEY

Within the trinity of spirit, soul, and body, we might consider the soul to be a two-sided magic mirror. The reincarnating soul is a reflection of our divine spirit, living in the highest regions of the infinite universe. As the soul incarnates into the material world—sent symbolically on a new earthly mission by the all-wise spirit—it chooses mental, emotional, and etheric-physical matter to clothe itself during the lifetime to come. This mental, emotional, and etheric-physical substance is a kind of reflection or mirror of the soul's accumulated knowledge, wisdom, and understanding.

Like spirit, soul, and body, the Sun, Moon, and Earth are a trinity. What is the Moon—which appears so often in fairy tales and throughout many of the Trumps within *Inner Child Cards*—other than a giant celestial mirror? It is the mirror of the Sun, waxing and waning as it changes its astronomical relationship to the Earth. The Moon is simultaneously a reflection of solar light, a nurturing mother throughout our lives, and a changing image of our growth in the world. The Moon is also the ruler of the tides and oceans, which are great reflectors (when calm) of the sky, clouds, and birds above, symbols of higher life. In astrology, the Moon is connected to the precious metal silver—the metal used to make mirrors!

In Jewish mysticism, the Kabbala holds the secret wisdom teachings of that ancient religion. Within the Kabbala is the mysterious Tree of Life, composed of four Sephirothic trees, each consisting of ten globes, in three columns, all linked by twenty-two pathways. While this Tree of

Life is very complex in nature, it contains within it a reflection or mirror of the human being—with its sacred chakras, primary organs, and multiple levels of consciousness. Like the Major Trumps—to which it is linked—the Kabbalist Tree of Life is a magic mirroring device, an intricate system to enter into the hidden knowledge of divine wisdom.

A great scholar of the tarot, Eliphas Levi, wrote in his book *Transcendental Magic* that "An imprisoned person, with no other book than the Tarot, if he knew how to use it, could in a few years acquire universal knowledge, and would be able to speak on all subjects with unequalled learning and inexhaustible eloquence." * Part of the reason this is true is that the Major Trumps, like individual mirrors, speak to us as pictures and fairy-tale stories. Like dreams, they are packed with symbolic meaning. Many investigators of occult knowledge believe that dreams occur not merely "in our heads," but in what is called "the astral realm." The astral world is like a cosmic sea in which we all bathe at night, a sea sometimes calmly reflecting our noblest efforts and other times reflecting our turbulent emotions. The astral realm is also a mirror reflection of spiritual life—so sometimes we discover distortions of higher truth in dreams while other times we receive cryptic messages filled with illuminating knowledge.

To understand more about the Major Trumps as a mirror, let us return to the imagery of the Tree of Life. Dr. Irene Gad, in her book *Tarot and Individuation*, says:

> In Lurianic cabalism (a 16th century school) it is taught that contemplating the sephirot (the ten emanations on the Tree of Life) with faith and hope promotes secret movements from above that evoke the inner lights

---

*Manly Palmer Hall, *The Secret Teachings of All Ages*, Diamond Jubilee Edition, Chapter XXIX, "An Analysis of the Tarot Cards" (Los Angeles: Philosophical Research Society, Inc.) 1988.

of each heavenly attribute and turn them toward the supplicating soul below. This perception of the full bliss of the Infinite exerts a beneficial influence, and one becomes conscious of the divine spirit embedded in one's soul. This revelation is represented by the descending Lightning Flash.*

The Tree of Life holds a very important story line in reference to the evolution of humanity for it serves as root knowledge. Fairy tales are similar in that they hold myriad characters and aspects of awakening in a pattern that is repeated and held in form over and over again. In a sense, the fairy story is a kind of root knowledge.

In many fairy tales, a tree plays a significant role in symbolizing different aspects of consciousness. The hazelnut tree is heard of again and again—usually in the form of a branch of one of these mystical trees. The hazelnut tree has a very short dormant period and thus is a life-giving tree. After only one month of losing its leaves, it begins to bloom again. In the story of Cinderella, the hazelnut tree watered with her tears grows to hold all the birds of the world who become her magical helpers. The tree stands for the root knowledge and heritage of her deceased mother coming back to her.

The Major Trumps stand like a great fertile tree among the flowering suits. They have stood solid and endured the test of time—just like fairy tales. The words and meanings may be altered, depending on who is telling the story. Yet a great history and integrity are still in place. Both fairy tales and the Major Arcana serve as mirrors to regain soul wisdom. The esoteric teaching of the tarot has to have been based on an oral tradition in order for it to have survived over the centuries. The same is true for fairy tales. They address the area of life where spirit and matter meet and serve as a bridge to unite the inner and outer worlds.

---

*Irene Gad, *Tarot and Individuation* (York Beach, Maine: Nicolas•Hays, 1994).

Hidden in the meaning of the Major Arcana cards is the step-by-step process of maturation that a human being must experience in a lifetime. Some are successful with it; many are not. Nevertheless, the potential is always there. Some souls have a very difficult time meeting the tasks of higher understanding and remain stuck in the lower worlds. These lower worlds are mostly the darkened aspects of fear, greed, lust, and many other maladies of the soul force. The Major Arcana serve as an archetypal guide and may comfort those who feel in exile or alienated from the roots of their origins. The power of these twenty-two Major Trumps is fierce and gentle at the same time. They can be considered the soul messengers within the seventy-eight cards of the tarot deck. When many Major cards appear in a session, I tell a client that his or her soul is speaking clearly and truthfully.

The richness and beauty of the Major Arcana is that it can serve humanity in two distinctive ways. On one level, the twenty-two cards represent a mirror of the divine and usually hidden aspects of our spiritual self. These are archetypes buried within the unconscious that may arise suddenly and awaken us, sometimes in a flash or unexpected awareness. The fairy tale functions in the same way. A sudden occurrence will enchant and create a moment when nothing will ever be the same again. The twenty-two Major cards also serve in a practical way. We can gain wisdom about the way we must move about the world according to a higher plan. When these cards show up in a reading, they can also offer a very specific way in which we are meant to make a choice or decision.

THE COURT CARDS: MAGIC MIRRORS

The sixteen court cards of tarot stand atop each suit almost as the Major Trumps are positioned over the fifty-six Minor Trumps. Initially named King, Queen, Jack, and Page back in the late 1300s and

1400s when tarot cards first appeared in European society, their current names within *Inner Child Cards* (Guardian, Guide, Seeker, and Child) are more representative of a modern world now disassociated from the ideas and trappings of royal families. However, it is instructive to go back six or seven hundred years to see how the court figures and the four suits that they rule mirrored the social scheme of that time period.

Drawing from historical sources, Manly Palmer Hall reminds us in *The Secret Teachings of All Ages* that with respect to countries, the "*kings* are their governments, the *queens* their religions, the *knights* their histories and national characteristics, and the *pages* their arts and sciences."*

Thus, there is a level of understanding of the court figures that goes beyond individual meaning and interpretation. They can refer to the mundane world and a powerful hierarchy of worldly activity.

Many researchers into the history of tarot have revealed that the four suits originally reflected four main classes within the society that existed when the cards surfaced in France. The cups—perhaps linked to the legends of the Holy Grail—stood for the priesthood. The swords—for obvious reasons—represented soldiers, armies, and military figures. The coins symbolized the emerging class of merchants and traders, while the flowering rods were connected with farmers. It is natural that over the centuries the four suits in the evolving tarot have changed to mirror the growth and evolution of society. This is very clearly done within the structure of the Minor Arcana in *Inner Child Cards*.

Court cards are very influential in helping us to understand ourselves and the people who live around us. They show us pictures of the archetypal qualities of the people in our life. It is very powerful

---

*Manly Palmer Hall, *The Secret Teachings of All Ages* Chapter XXIX, "An Analysis of the Tarot Cards."

to see a court card in the relationship part of a reading, for this will often be a picture of the main person now energizing a person's intimate life. There is a position in some layouts that shows us how we feel about ourselves; a court card here is potent as we get to see a clear image of what personality forces are at work deep within. The court cards have a unique quality shown by the fact that they are the only ones not numbered. They are more like living values of humanity and the various stages of growth that we encounter. Where the Major Arcana cards are like the big picture to the soul, the court cards are the little picture—the personal view, the identity awareness within the larger arena of soul discovery.

The court cards are key players in a personal reading for many reasons. They serve as the significator if one chooses to use this form of divination. One will choose a court card figure that looks most like or represents the quality of the person. The Winged Hearts would be used to signify a person who possesses great love and is very generous, kind and feeling-oriented, and for someone who may be experiencing emotional healing at this stage in life. The Sword of Truth would be used for someone of mental origins, who is very intelligent, rational, or clear, and one whose mission is to promote higher learning. The Magic Wands would be chosen to signify a person who is opening the channels of intuition and spirituality. The person would be passionate and creative—vibrant, alive, and fiery. The Earth Crystals would be used to represent a person who is practical, abundant, very connected to nature and earth awareness. This person could also be active in business or sales, associated with money and material success. The significator is the first card in the reading and is often chosen face up, used as a mirror to the person who is receiving the reading. Many people do not choose a significator, but, if they do, they will choose a court card.

Each suit of the Minor Arcana has four court cards, but in modern playing cards, there are only three in each suit—Jack, Queen, and

King. The missing card is the Page or the Child in *Inner Child Cards*. Why is the Page missing? Could it be the same reason the Major Arcana cards, except for The Fool as The Joker, are missing? It's as if the mirror of our higher journey in life—the spiritual pilgrimage that exists beyond our material accomplishments—has been taken away from us the last few hundred years, a time filled with environmental pollution, societal degeneration, and world wars. We have only a distorted figure left—the mocking Joker—to link us back to the hallowed ground of the Major Arcana. Similarly, the Page holds the mystical inner vision of the innocent soul. The Child is still pure, one who must learn to be open and receive before action is taken. When we see a Child or Page in the tarot, we know the individual is embarking upon a new journey, about to move forward on a path of mastery and authority. The first stage is to understand the inner message. This is the listening or receptive stage. The Western world is not accustomed to this stage of life and does not warmly embrace the notion of archetypal inner myth and stories unless they are directed at little children. Could the missing cards be an indicator that the Western world has lost touch with its soul? I would say yes.

THE NUMERICAL CARDS: EVERYDAY ENCOUNTERS

While the forty numerical cards of the Minor Arcana symbolize more of our everyday existence than the life-changing epiphanies that occur rarely in a human life, they are by no means insignificant. It is the split-second decisions we make each day and the numerous encounters we have with other people that determine our primary destiny. Every Minor card carries a number vibration and numbers are the foundation of the universe! It has often been said that the divine intelligence that has created all of life has done so through geometry, sound, and number. Language itself—and each letter of a language—carries a numerical vibration. Within the communication that allows human society to exist as a coherent and interactive species is hidden the power of numbers *one* through *nine*.

One aspect of understanding the deeper significance of the tarot is to become aware of the meaning of a number vibration. When you choose a numerical card, you must first understand the energetic quality of the suit. Is the card part of the water-ruled suit (a Winged Heart), the air-ruled suit (a Sword of Truth), the fire-ruled suit (a Magic Wand), or the earth-ruled suit (an Earth Crystal)? These elemental energies tell us about the different temperaments and states of consciousness that a person contains within. Once you understand this, you can move to the number value. Within the suits, the numerical cards show us several aspects: the level of activity; the way we should go about resolving conflict in life; how to organize our life in a better way; or the movement from one stage to another. For example, every ace (1) represents a new start that will not reach completion until the ninth card of the suit is reached. It is only in the shift from 9 to 10 (liberation) that one's evolution carries one back to the ace (10 = 1 + 0 = 1) and to a new beginning.

In addition to the fascinating pictures and stories, each reading has messages to give in the number qualities linking various cards. Above and beyond each numerical card is a Major Arcana numbered card. Thus not only will every ace (1) symbolize a beginning, rebirth, and new gift, but it will also link to Aladdin and the Magic Lamp (I), Alice in Wonderland (X), and The Yellow Brick Road (XIX). Combining these keynotes can often prove fascinating. For instance, with the above three Major Arcana cards, the keynotes are as follows: The Creative Child (I), The Wheel of Life (X), and The Cosmic Self (XIX).

The qualities of numbers have been studied in depth by numerologists. Most numerologists owe their understanding to Pythagoras, the great Greek sage who first coined the term *philosopher* over 2,500 years ago. Pythagoras—while a real person—has taken on legendary and mythic proportions over the more than twenty-five centuries since he established an esoteric school of knowledge in Crotona, Southern Italy. While much of the educational curriculum of this school has been lost, several authors—including Thomas Taylor in his book *The Theoretic Arithmetic of the Pythagoreans*—have put together ideas of the extensive numerical wizardry that Pythagoras and his disciples studied more than 500 years before the birth of Jesus. Pythagoras thought of numbers much differently than even the numerologists of the modern era. To some extent, numbers *one* and *two* were considered more as the Father and Mother energies, the Monad and the Duad. As the forces of unity and duality, they were not really considered numbers in the same way as *three*, *four*, *five*, etc. To assist you in interpreting the basic values of numbers, the following ideas have been culled from various sources on numerology. It is important to realize that the science of numbers is steeped in an incredibly rich tradition and to truly understand the mystical power of numbers you should study the original texts.

Basic Values of Numbers

One: unity; divinity; wholeness; source; integration; singular; isolation; the point

Two: division; separation; duality; marriage; partnership; polarity; receptivity; the line

Three: creativity; justice; virtue; vision; wisdom and understanding; the surface

Four: foundation; form; strength; earthly power; harmony through conflict; the solid

Five: light; health; vitality; mental power; inspiration; change; spiritual growth

Six: balance; perfection; equilibrium; divine love; loyalty; resolution of conflict

Seven: the sacred; mystical; imagination; synthesis; psychic; dreams and visions

Eight: emotional power; resistance; prudence; law; regeneration; determination; will

Nine: conclusion; adventure; striving; hope; courage; selflessness; embryonic growth

Ten: perfection; attainment; completion; accomplishment; authority; leadership

Chapter 6

Additional Ways to Use the Inner Child Cards

Over the past nine years since *Inner Child Cards* were first published, we have received inspiring mail from many people around the world who have found new and exciting ways to use the cards in therapy, tarot sessions, schools, past-life regression sessions, and many other modalities that we could not have anticipated. People of all ages and nationalities respond to the cards and there are many ways to use them. Although I have not personally witnessed other people's work with the cards, I have sought to integrate some of the ideas that have come to me from others into my own practice and work with clients. Some therapists use the cards as free pictures for their clients to sort through at random, choosing the images that best speak to specific issues as they arise. They are also wonderful to use in Inner Child groups, in therapy groups, at births, at gatherings of various sorts, and at birthday parties.

I would like to tell you of one of my own experiences, but before I do, let me share a secret with you. The faces of my and Mark's two daughters and ourselves were each painted into one of the *Inner Child Cards*; the card that depicts me is the Guardian of Crystals known as Gaia. On my fortieth birthday, I had a gathering of women at my home. I placed *Inner Child Cards* on the floor around a candle-lit mandala of my life journey up to that point. As my women friends sang and chanted, I circled around the beautiful candles and the cards, which were face down, preparing to choose my "true" birth-day card for my fortieth year and my fifth decade. When the time felt right, I bent down to select a card at random, and lo and behold, I chose myself—The Guardian of Crystals! This was a funny and moving moment for my friends and me and further empowered the synchronicity of the tarot for all of us. The cards are potent, and if used with reverence and care, they will serve you, your family, and your clients in extraordinary ways.

PAST-LIFE REGRESSION

I have found the cards extremely useful in helping people understand the roots of their incarnation. For a Past-Life Regression reading, I have used a modification of The Child layout to indicate the origins of the individual's soul, as well as the destiny plan he or she is here to engage with. As described in detail in *Inner Child Cards*, five cards are placed in a row, each card representing one letter of the word *child*. The same correlation between the letters applies. However, the em-phasis in a Past-Life Regression is more on the soul birth and the karmic imprints the individual is clearing and healing. The first card, stand-ing for the letter C, indicates the past-life circumstance or imprint that the individual needs to work with and resolve. The second card, standing for the letter H, shows the aspirant's highest potential in dealing with the incarnation issue. The third card, standing for the letter I, represents the incarnation instead of representing identity as it does in The Child reading. This perspective holds a much broader view of the universality of the individual's soul journey. This card is crucial, for it mirrors an absolute image of potential to the individual.

The fourth card, standing for the letter *L*, represents lessons from the past and perhaps a picture of a lesson that is being very much brought to the surface in this lifetime. Finally, the fifth card, standing for the letter *D*, indicates one's destiny, as well as the best way to work with and resolve the karmic conditions.

Sometimes the situation will not appear to be a challenge. Remember to observe carefully, however. It is entirely possible that there is a lesson or a challenge to be learned from the cards—though I do not subscribe to the notion that a reversed card necessarily indicates some sort of reversal or obstacle in one's life. When attempting to discern the deepest and broadest possible meaning of the cards, it is important to examine how the image communicates to the soul. For instance, if the Two of Winged Hearts appears in the C position, it might be reasonable to assume that there is an issue regarding relationships in this lifetime. How then will the issue be resolved and dealt with in the highest fashion? The future cards will reveal this and offer a real solution. Listen with your soul and try to take full advantage of the wisdom being offered through this medium.

In a deep healing session, an individual is often very sensitive to sensory stimuli such as sound and voice tones, color, and scent. This may be why *Inner Child Cards* have proven so successful an aid in regression work. The colors stimulate the senses and the images are dreamy. They pull one forward into the terrain of another world. It has been truly amazing what individuals have seen in the cards with reference to their own life experience and healing.

For example, I once worked with a young woman who had been sexually abused by her father. I asked her if she would like to choose an image from the deck to illuminate her process. She chose the Eight of Winged Hearts. That card depicts a very powerful harmonic event between two figures of the opposite sex. In *Inner Child*

Cards, this image denotes a fusion of energy either within the individual or with another. It heralds a metamorphosis—a new soul pattern emerging. As the young woman looked into this card, she saw something there that I had never seen before. She brought to my attention the fact that the two tails of the mermaid and merman come together to create a beautiful green butterfly. For this astute woman, the symbol indicated that she had been set free from the bondage of her father's past actions. Tears flowed as we enjoyed the liberating archetype of the butterfly, with all of its ramifications for healing. Through this process, the young woman came to a very deep and forgiving place.

Another time I was working with a different young woman who had experienced not only sexual abuse but battering as well. She had often witnessed violence in her home and been deeply traumatized by the experience. Our session focused on her healing, and after a tremendous amount of hard emotional work on her part, the young woman decided she would like to choose an *Inner Child Card*. Her chosen card was The Guardian Angel, a beautiful message in itself. Again, however, my client saw something unique in the card that spoke to her own heart. Upon noticing the white rose held by the Guardian Angel, this young woman began to cry, explaining that the only time she felt safe in her home was when her father would bring her mother white roses after a battle the previous night. In this way, the white roses came to symbolize hope for her. The Guardian Angel of *Inner Child Cards* offered my client a white rose, reminding her that there was hope in her healing process and suggesting that this was a turning point for her.

Young children—still very open to the imagination and memory of their origins—may be helped by *Inner Child Cards* to tap into the core of their creativity. Have the cards arched in a beautiful rainbow shape and ask the child to go to the rainbow and choose a special picture. Then ask the child what they see and how the person in the picture is feeling. Ask the child to put their own face into the picture and then ask them how they feel and what is happening. Often this will trigger imagination and some very revealing stories. You do not need to discuss the details with them. Write the child's observations and save them for when they are older, so that they may read the stories of their soul, or, if the child is a client, offer these precious stories to the parents so that they may understand the inner life of the child. (Of course, this should only be done in cases where one is not breaking confidentiality.)

DREAMWORK

Dreams are a reflection of our inner life. Consequently, dream images are very important in helping us understand the unconscious as it moves upward into conscious understanding. We take our busy lives to bed with us each night and the experiences of each day are reflected in our dreams. If you are choosing to remember your dreams and interpret them, you might consider making it a priority each night to ask that your dreams become messengers for your highest good and serve as a teacher along the path of awakening.

I often suggest to my clients that they choose an image from *Inner Child Cards* that they feel will assist them with their night's journey. Placing this card alongside the bed stand or even under your pillow can be a lovely and powerful protection and aid. For children this is especially true if the card is The Guardian Angel or The Fairy Godmother. For adults, many cards are appropriate and useful.

Sometimes a client will want to share a recent dream with me. After recounting the dream, we often will look at *Inner Child Cards* for clues to the healing that the dream is trying to facilitate. This is a way to take the dream to the next step and it is always incredible to observe the result.

INNER CHILD CARDS RUMMY

Four to Eight Players.

(The more players you have, the longer the game will take.)

In our historical study of the tarot, we often read about the possibility that the cards were used as a game. Some suggest this was a way of hiding the mystical content of the cards, a way for the cards to be in the hands of the layperson without fear of persecution. We know that many card games stem from the practice of the tarot and that cards have been a source of enjoyment and attunement for people through the ages. In that spirit, I would like to offer a way of playing cards with the tarot deck that was introduced to me by Mary Greer, author of *Tarot for Yourself*, as well as by many other valuable books of depth and innovation. The game is great fun, so I hope you will share it with family and friends.

Take the entire tarot deck and pass it around the circle so that each person can shuffle the cards. The dealer will deal as many cards to each person as there are players in the game. Thus, if there are four players, each player will receive four cards, five players five cards, and so on. Taking turns, each player will offer a tarot card to each of the other players. With four players, three cards will be given out to the three other players and one card will be kept for oneself. As each player offers a card, he or she explains why that card is being given to the chosen player. The dealer begins by choosing a person to offer a card to. That chosen person will go next and each person who is given a card will be the next to offer a card. The game continues until all people once again have four cards—three gift cards from the other players and one card that they have kept for themselves. This is a game that offers insights, gifts, and affirmations to each person. In a way, it is like a group tarot reading with everyone offering and receiving messages throughout the game. This game is great for a women's or men's group and wonderful for family members or friends to play in order to gain mutual understanding and trust.

Chapter 7

New Layouts

I hope you will enjoy the new layouts in the *Inner Child Cards Workbook*. These are layouts I have been using with clients over the years that are not in the original book. Remember to choose your intended layout before shuffling the cards with sensitivity and care. Then fan the cards, face down, and select the required number with your left hand, placing each card face down in its position.

THE DYNAMIC STAR LAYOUT

Down through the ages, the star has been recognized as one of the most profound shapes in nature. Reflecting the movement of Venus in the heavens, it constitutes the shape of all five-petal flowers, including the rose and fruit flowers such as apples, pears, plums, and apricots. The branches of these trees have been used as magic wands, totems, and ceremonial objects in cultures the world over. The energetic patterning of the star mirrors the five points of the human body, comprised of the four limbs and the head, as diagramed in the famous Leonardo da Vinci sketch of man. The star represents myriad potentials and helps us to understand the movement of time and space, the inner and outer worlds, and the balance of change and chaos. The potential to understand the balance of freedom and form is within the numerological power of the number *five*.

The Dynamic Star layout represents a tiny replica of the human body wherein each limb and the crown point pertain to a particular area of life. This layout helps an individual synthesize the various areas or branches of his or her life and allows greater clarity to arise out of whatever changes are taking place.

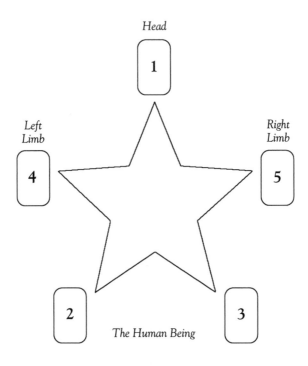

The Dynamic Star Layout

After shuffling the deck and fanning out the cards, choose five cards and place them face down into the pattern as indicated in the drawing. The star represents yourself *looking back toward you*—head above, feet below, with the right side of your body the positive, active pole of life and the left side of your body the negative, receptive pole of life. As you draw each card, consider the following themes for each placement.

Card 1: spiritual center; the third eye; seeking higher vision and truth

Card 2: stepping forward in the world and on your life path

Card 3: in-reach and in-breath emotionally; tuning into your heart's desire; grasping and holding on to what's important for you to learn

Card 4: out-reach and out-breath emotionally; focusing on your goals and how to attain them; offering your hand in friendship to others and support for those in need

Card 5: stepping backward to review and synthesize your experiences and achievements

THE REBIRTH LAYOUT

The Rebirth Layout is a seven-card layout that spells the word *rebirth*. The number *seven* is a transformational number, signifying spiritual return to the original home. Trump card number VII is traditionally The Chariot. In *Inner Child Cards*, it is Peter Pan, symbolizing a reawakening to the magical qualities of the soul and balancing them in everyday life.

Fan out entire deck.

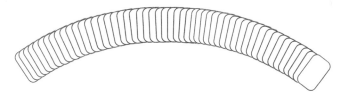

Choose seven cards and lay them out in order spelling the word *rebirth*.

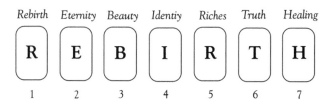

The Rebirth Layout

Each letter signifies a particular energy of self-realization and healing. As you turn each card over you will discover the path of evolution your new self has embarked upon.

Card 1, the letter R: This card is a picture of your Rebirth. This position reveals the new qualities you have discovered within yourself that you are now ready to express in the world.

Card 2, the letter E: This card represents Eternity. This position represents the aspect of your soul that has been with you for many lifetimes and is now available to you in its highest form. This Eternal quality will never abandon you. You have rediscovered it and you must cherish it throughout the duration of your lifetime.

Card 3, the letter B: This card represents the Beauty of your soul and the way it is being reflected in the world today.

Card 4, the letter I: This is the Identity of the soul. In this layout, your newly emerging Identity is being shown to you: the new you. This is similar to the role of the letter *I* in The Child layout where it also appears in the central position, emphasizing the pivotal theme of ego awareness and self-reflection.

Card 5, the letter R: This card reveals the Riches you now have to offer the world.

Card 6, the letter T: This card reveals the Truth you may now freely express through word, deed, and action.

Card 7, the letter H: This card reveals the Healing that is offered to you as you embark upon the path toward Higher Consciousness.

With the help of the Rebirth Layout, many of my clients have done remarkable work in reclaiming their self-worth and embracing the life they are meant to live. It often feels as if they are being born into a new dimension of consciousness and many of them feel as though they are being reincarnated in this lifetime without having to shed their body and start all over again. Not only do I observe an inner shift that changes the mental constructs characteristic of the person, but I also observe a physical difference in the way they move their body and express themselves through movement.

THE ARCHETYPE LAYOUT: MIRROR, MIRROR ON THE WALL

Fan out twenty-two cards from the Major Arcana in an oval. Choose one card and place it upright in the middle of the oval. This is your mirror.

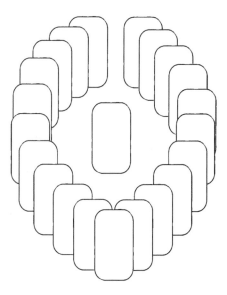

The Archetype Layout: Mirror, Mirror on the Wall

This is a simple layout with profound implications. The Archetype layout serves as a true mirror of your inner being, allowing you to understand the archetypal energies you are identifying with at this time in your life.

Our relationships, lifestyles, opportunities, successes, and failures all reflect our inner consciousness. In this way, the world mirrors our inner selves back to us. The image of The Empress in the *Mother Peace Tarot,* by Vickie Noble, is a beautiful depiction of this aspect of reality. The Empress, representing our earthly riches and physical life, holds up a mirror. She doesn't look directly into it, but rather holds it outward, toward nature, symbolizing her ultimate connection to the natural world and her instinctual self. She accepts that she is an interpretation, or mirror, of the world as she chooses to see it.

In the tale of Snow White, the wicked queen is a representation of this metaphysical law. Her inner life is corrupted by greed and jealousy. Her heart is not pure and her intentions are not of the highest. She represents the static state of fear and darkness that governs the world of the individual until the willingness to release these painful patterns finally takes center stage. Humanity is blessed with free will, and, with it, the ability to grow beyond our shortcomings and shortsightedness. Fairy tales reflect the universal desire to overcome all obstacles and persevere in the quest for ultimate freedom.

For this reading, first separate the twenty-two rainbow-edged Major Arcana cards from the rest of the deck. You will be using them as a mini-deck. These Major Arcana cards serve as especially potent archetypal mirrors to humanity. Spread the cards face down in a circle, so that each card is visible. It is best if you lay out the cards on a lovely piece of fabric or tablecloth. As you gaze upon the circular mirror you have created, ask that a true and perfect reflection of your inner consciousness be revealed. Choose a card and place it face up in the center of the circle. There you are!

I offer this exercise to my clients after a session where they have been able to identify old patterns and behaviors and have seen beyond them, even if only for a moment. At such times, The Archetype reading can be very healing and informative.

THE YELLOW BRICK ROAD LAYOUT

Often, in my talks and lectures on the use of *Inner Child Cards,* I have referred to the evolutionary path of the tarot as the Yellow Brick Road to Consciousness. Each step forward on the ancient, twenty-two-card, mystical path leads one nearer to his or her true nature, just as Dorothy journeyed down the Yellow Brick Road, eventually finding her way home.

As with The Archetype layout, use only the Major Arcana cards. Out of them, select five cards to be placed in a row, representing the archetypal seekers, Dorothy, the Scarecrow, the Tin Man, and the Lion, as well as the Yellow Brick Road.

Fan out the twenty-two Major Arcana cards.

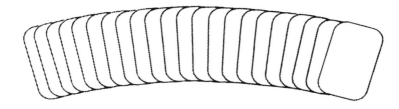

Choose five cards and lay them out in order.

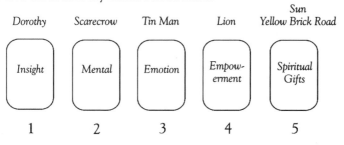

Dorothy	Scarecrow	Tin Man	Lion	Sun Yellow Brick Road
Insight	Mental	Emotion	Empowerment	Spiritual Gifts
1	2	3	4	5

The Yellow Brick Road Layout

Imagine yourself on a magical journey, traveling the Yellow Brick Road toward your inner light. Each position is a stepping-stone in the direction of your true nature, as these beloved characters come to life within your own psyche. Allow them to inform you about the ways you manage your dreams, your mental thoughts, your emotions, your strength, and your courage, as you seek the ultimate treasure of self.

In this layout, **the first card** represents Dorothy, the Seeker of Wands, the part of us that has embarked upon a new dream or vision. What is this insight?

The second card is the Scarecrow, the Seeker of Swords, the part of us that is forever seeking truth and clarity. This card indicates the way in which you use your mental skills. Do you honor your ability to make decisions?

The third card is the Tin Man, the Seeker of Hearts, the part of us that learns through the path of the heart. This card reveals the way you respond to your emotions and inner world of feelings. Are you able to receive love?

The fourth card is the Cowardly Lion, the Seeker of Crystals, the part of us that holds pride and honor in the physical world. This card reflects the way you empower yourself with self-confidence and courage. Are you able to accomplish your dreams?

The fifth and final card is The Sun card. In *Inner Child Cards*, Trump number XIX, The Sun, is symbolized by the Yellow Brick Road. In this card we see Dorothy and her three companions traveling the path of destiny, toward the Emerald City, where the Wizard of Oz resides. The Wizard offers Dorothy and her friends that which they already possess, the pure riches that reside within each of them. You see, The Sun or Yellow Brick Road is not a destination but a lived experience, reflecting one's true nature. This card reveals the spiritual gifts that are yours forevermore. They were never really lost, and now that they are remembered, they become a conscious part of your life from this day forward.

Chapter 8

The Twenty-Two Major Arcana

As mentioned in earlier chapters, the twenty-two Major Arcana cards are the soul of a seventy-eight-card tarot deck. These cards—representing various archetypes, energy fields, and character traits embedded within the consciousness of humanity—have been described as the evolutionary road to spiritual illumination. Numbered from zero to twenty-one, the cards that create the Major Arcana serve as stepping-stones or initiations that lead one toward new levels of insight from a mystical, psychological, and spiritual perspective.

Individuals who are studying and using the tarot as a means toward personal growth may cycle through different numerical positions of the Major Arcana depending on what stage of development they have arrived at on their own Royal Road to Wisdom—be it spiritual, emotional, physical, or mental. One person may find a mirror in the Hermit card—calling for an inner journey into the caverns of self-exploration. The Fool might beckon another individual toward new beginnings and the unexpected.

When choosing cards or a card from a face-down position, one is allowing the law of synchronicity to play a part in the individual's soul message. Whether one chooses one, two, three cards or more, this chapter will explain the significance of the Major Arcana card or cards as they appear to you as a mirror of personal reflection.

Following an inspiring quote, the information for each card is broken down into five categories as follows:

Traditional Meaning: This section offers the reader a definition of the card that stems out of traditional tarot interpretation. For hundreds of years the tarot images have maintained an integrity that is rooted in their ancient imagery and symbolism. In order to gain a pure and in-depth interpretation of the cards, it is helpful to understand the card from this vantage point before delving into the *Inner Child Cards* fairy-tale correlation. This will help an individual grasp the whole meaning of the card—allowing for a balance of imagination and practical application.

Keywords: The words offered in this section are to be used as a quick and direct way of understanding the image chosen. These words are intended to give a clear focus regarding the nature of the card.

Fairy-Tale Lore: This section describes the fairy-tale correlation that has been associated with the Major Arcana card. It complements the information given in the guidebook that accompanies *Inner Child Cards*. Additional symbolism implied in each fairy tale is offered so that you may connect this source of wisdom to your own life with clarity and imagination.

Questions and Affirmations: These sections offer reflection and inquiry through questions and affirmations as a way to help you understand and clarify the card's meaning elaborated in the sections on traditional meaning, keywords, and fairy-tale lore. Through meditation, writing, or sharing thoughts and ideas with friends and loved ones, these questions and affirmations may clear the way for a broader perspective on how each card relates to your personal life. What is the card asking of you? What do you need to understand about your life at this time? The questions and affirmations offer an interactive relationship with the cards that is also beneficial as you learn to read the cards for others with confidence and clarity.

Little Red Cap

O
LITTLE RED CAP:
THE FOOL

*"Her grandmother loved her best of all,
and was always thinking what she could
do for the child. One day she made her a
present of a red velvet cap, and because
it was so becoming to the little girl, who
would wear nothing else, she was called
by everyone 'Little Red Cap.'"*

—"Little Red Cap," *Grimm's
Fairy Tales,* 1891

Traditional Meaning

In the traditional tarot, Little Red Cap is Trump 0 (The Fool). The
Fool is the proverbial genius and mirrors the potential for new growth
and individuation. Often pictured is a young lad, standing at the
edge of a jagged cliff, with one foot dangling out beyond the firm
earth. A dog barks and nips at his heels, for the task of awakening is
at hand and the dog will represent one of two options depending on
the consciousness of the individual—either caution or primal courage. The Fool has a responsibility. As Trump 0 he can take great
leaps of faith toward a future potential.

Keywords

Surprise; shock; sudden change; movement beyond the known to
the unknown; leap of faith.

Fairy-Tale Lore

Little Red Cap was instructed by her mother *not* to veer from the path on her way to her grandmother's house. This force in the story represents the child's origins, her past, and the form that Little Red Cap must liberate from in order to move along the path of maturation. She is cloaked in red, a color that exposes her to her own fires of transformation and awakening. Along the path Little Red Cap meets the Big Bad Wolf who distracts her from her course. She becomes dazzled by the sun's rays playing amongst the flowers of the meadow and decides to pick a bouquet for her grandmother. From the child's enchantment with nature a test is being summoned by her soul. Once she arrives at her grandmother's house she again meets the Wolf (the shadow) in disguise (how often is our shadow disguised from our own ignorance?). She is gobbled up by the hungry Wolf. A huntsman venturing through the woods is curious to hear loud snoring coming out of the grandmother's cottage. There he recognizes the Wolf as an old nemesis that he has wanted to conquer (the shadow has been recognized). The huntsman cuts open the belly of the Wolf or the womb of rebirth—0, The Fool's primordial egg—to free Little Red Cap and her grandmother. The awakening of the soul has occurred and in the future Little Red Cap will be more aware of what lurks in the forest. In older tales, Little Red Cap meets the Wolf three times; each time she is more able to outsmart him. One tale ends as Little Red Cap and her grandmother trick the Wolf by leading him into a pot of boiling sausage. This transformation theme is played out in other tales such as "The Three Little Pigs" and *The Wizard of Oz*.

Questions

What is ready to be set free and reborn within my life?
What aspects of the future call out to me?
How can I make my life more passionate and free?

Affirmations

I am ready to let go of the past and set my life free.
I cast my shadow to the light and open to new possibilities.

Aladdin & the Magic Lamp

I
ALADDIN AND THE MAGIC LAMP: THE MAGICIAN

"To Mercury or Hermes (Hiram) the Egyptians attributed their forty-two books of science, embracing astronomy, astrology, arithmetic, geometry, medicine, grammar, logic, rhetoric, music, magic, and so on. Mercury or Hermes was the great magician and transformer, bearing the caduceus, or wand of miracles, which survives to this day as a symbol of the healing art. He was, nevertheless, only the messenger of a divinity higher than himself—merely the transmitter, not the originator, the channel rather than the source."

—Paul Foster Case, *The Tarot: A Key to the Wisdom of the Ages*

Traditional Meaning

In many decks, a magician is seen standing before a table on which are placed the four elemental qualities in the form of a chalice, a sword, a pentacle, and a rod, symbolizing water, air, earth, and fire. A garden of flowers is in front of the table while a vine often appears near the top of the card. This is a person who is connected with growth. Usually he is a representation of Mercury, the divine messenger of the gods, from ancient Greek mythology. As such, he symbolizes a mediator between heaven and earth. If he is focused, clear of mind, and conscientious, he will be able to utilize all the best resources that the world has to offer to carry out a successful mission—whether in the arts, science, business, a trade, or professional work. Sometimes the image of infinity (a figure eight on its side) is seen over his head while his belt is a serpent biting its own tail (eternity). Both of these reflect the idea that this individual is endowed with celestial wisdom. To further reinforce this reality, his right hand (pointing upward) may be grasping a wand while his left hand points to the ground. His complete image suggests a lightning-bolt and that he—as an expression of the animus (the male psychological archetype in nature)—can be an awakener, guiding you to higher truth and arcane knowledge.

Keywords

Control; skill; faith in oneself; animus; channeling; divine messenger; scientific genius.

Fairy-Tale Lore

In "Aladdin and the Magic Lamp," we find a far more satisfying story than that of The Magician. While the traditional representation is a potent one—filled with esoteric symbols and a dynamic potency—the rich imagery of a young boy exploring his mental potential with the aid of an all-powerful genie is truly profound. Don't be fooled by the genders portrayed. Since this is a card of discovering the magical nature of your imagination as a creative force, feel free to experiment by turning the figures into a young girl and female genie. While there is a tendency to identify with Aladdin when this card appears in a reading, realize that every facet of this trump is YOU. Therefore, play around with the notion that you embody the genie. What higher intellectual or intuitive powers can you summon right now to turn your life around in a remarkable way? Perhaps a new, daily affirmation or way of thinking will give you the energetic boost you have been missing. It's also possible that in the real world, you are facing a crucial decision. The appearance of this card indicates you need to be mentally sharp, in complete control of your faculties, able to be the dominant person in a group, demonstrating total mastery of your subject and the skills needed to be fully successful. Remember that since Aladdin is also a child, the presence of this card may be asking you to plunge into a new project with strength, vitality, and youthful exuberance. To be enthusiastic is to be filled with the spirit of divinity; the word *enthusiastic* comes from *en-theos* (God).

Questions

What tools of my trade, resources of my business, or aspects of my professional life have been ignored or need reinforcement?

How can I grow and evolve my talent for . . . ?

When the lamp of consciousness is turned on, what do I see illuminated in my mind?

Affirmations

I am building my world on the magic contained within the four elements.

"I think, therefore I am."

The Fairy Godmother

II
THE FAIRY GODMOTHER: THE HIGH PRIESTESS

"Little tame doves, little turtle doves, and all the birds of heaven, come and help me pick up the seeds."

—"Cinderella," *Grimm's Fairy Tales*, 1891

Traditional Meaning

The High Priestess is the fertile, receptive, and intuitive force of the Divine Feminine. She waters the soul with her cosmic attunement and insight. Always open to receiving the powers of vision and higher truth, The High Priestess is representative of the balance of creation, for it is with her all-seeing eye and insight that we, on the Royal Road to Wisdom, will find our truest spiritual gifts. She embodies divine love and helps us to foster the qualities that will nurture this within our own life.

Keywords

Reflection; visualization; intuition; weaving the mysteries of nature with her magical visions.

Fairy-Tale Lore

In *Inner Child Cards*, The High Priestess is The Fairy Godmother. In the original version of "Cinderella," the Fairy Godmother is represented by the heavenly birds that live in Cinderella's Tree of Life. These beautiful helpers have come to assist Cinderella in her greatest time of need. They offer her faith and hope for they are the sweet reward that comes to her after her trials of suffering and service. She does not complain, but she knows there is a goal of empowerment that she will move toward. The Fairy Godmother comes alive as a force as the principle of universal love that will shower Cinderella with new vision and opportunity. The force of that principle is alive within the young child for her tears have become the deep work of her soul that will eventually prepare her to manifest her dreams.

Questions

Am I able to hear the messages of my heart?

If I took time each day to water my own garden of spiritual destiny, what would I love to do the most?

What are the visions in my life that I must focus on in order that my creations come to full fruition?

Affirmations

I am protected by the love of the Divine Mother that overlights me each and every day.

I listen to my heart's desires for these are the messages of divine purpose and creativity.

The heavens above shine down the beauty of my highest potentials.

Mother Goose

III
MOTHER GOOSE:
THE EMPRESS

"A sense of Her also comes through vision: through sights of great beauty. I have felt her when I see what we call [in] the Woodlands a Jesus-God sunset. I have felt her move in me from seeing the fishermen come up from the lake at dusk with lanterns lit, and also from seeing my newborn baby's toes all lined up like a row of sweet corn. We see Her where we see Her, which is everywhere."

—Clarissa Pinkola Estes,
Women Who Run with the Wolves

Traditional Meaning

The Empress, or Queen of the World, opens us to life that constantly renews itself. Mother Goose has a basket of eggs in her lap in *Inner Child Cards* representing spiritual rebirth and the incarnation of the soul. In The Empress card, the feminine principle is self-aware, intelligent, and conscious of its goals. She is the Trinity of the Holy Feminine, representing the Sun, Moon, and Earth—the spiritual, emotional, and physical self. The Empress is manifestation at the most sublime and aesthetic level. She is a mirror of divine creation; she is Natura, the queen of nature, who speaks to us through the language of the flowers, trees, mountains, forests, and heavens. She weaves her story through the fabric of our very own bodies.

Keywords

Fertility; creativity; wisdom of the earth; she is the force of nature that can bring about ideal forms.

Fairy-Tale Lore

In fairy tales and fables, birds often represent messengers and helpers from the spiritual world. Mother Goose is seen riding on her magical goose symbolizing mediation between heaven and earth.

Mother Goose in fairy-tale rhyme and riddle ignites our imagination, which inspires us to create language that shapes the inner reality of children and adults alike. We sing her songs into our soul life and, as we do, we strengthen the rapture and passion of our own creative imagination.

Questions

What new treasures am I birthing in my life at this time?
In what way does The Empress, Mother Goose, mirror my own life destiny?

Affirmations

I am a reflection of the bounty of nature; each day my life is colored by the potentials hidden within the magic eggs in Mother Goose's basket. The story of my life unfolds in perfect timing as I manifest the dream of my life.

IV

THE EMPEROR'S NEW CLOTHES: THE EMPEROR

The Emperor's New Clothes

"The emperor walked in the procession under his crimson canopy. And all the people of the town, who had lined the streets or were looking down from the windows, said the emperor's clothes were beautiful. None of them were willing to admit that they hadn't seen a thing; for if anyone did, then he was either stupid or unfit for the job he held. Never before had the emperor's clothes been such a success. 'But he doesn't have anything on!' cried a little child. 'Listen to the innocent one,' said the proud father."

—Hans Christian Andersen,
"The Emperor's New Clothes"

Traditional Meaning

In the traditional tarot, The Emperor represents the potential to build and construct, attain earthly power, and solidify the vision of the proceeding card, The Empress. He is associated with leadership, authority, management, and order. He stands for vital energy and—if the energy is used correctly—a strong healthy ego. The Emperor seeks to regulate and balance the social order and business of society. He is given responsibility and trust by others to do so. The test of The Emperor is to use his power and strength with grace and good will and to be honest in all of his dealings.

The number *four* is associated with fixed ideas and denotes a strong foundation or form to work from. At this juncture on the

Royal Road to Wisdom, we find an individual seeking harmony and union with authority and power. This is the most material of all cards. The following cards on the Royal Road seek to balance the stately and uniformed Emperor with refinement and spiritual attunement. The challenge The Emperor is offered lies within the way in which he responds to the needs of the greater community. He must remain open to truth and humility; otherwise, he will fall prey to scandal, lies, and deceit as in "The Emperor's New Clothes."

Keywords

Building; construction; form; divinity anchored on earth; the four-square world; order; mechanical law.

Fairy-Tale Lore

In *Inner Child Cards* we see a rather comical rendition of The Emperor; however, it is quite profound. The story of "The Emperor's New Clothes" serves as a metaphor that may reflect the conditions we face in our world today and offers the healing we may derive from being guided by its candid and humorous simplicity. A danger is indicated if The Emperor has lost touch with the nurturing presence of the feminine, for it is this divine presence that offers balance and harmony to the authority that The Emperor represents. The violation of power that The Emperor could be party to is not restricted to men, for both women and men have become victims of greed and materialism.

The Emperor is swindled by two cunning tailors anxious to attain monetary rewards. By seducing The Emperor with compliments and glamour, the tailors fool him into believing that they are designing garments of richness and ornamentation for him, when, in fact, they cunningly wrap him only in the myriad illusions that the tailors represent. As The Emperor enters the gates of the city, outfitted—or outwitted—in the bedazzling garments of trickery, the crowd cheers, blindly accepting the folly of their leader. The townspeople have lost touch with their ability to see truth and see only what they think they see. In the distance, a little child in the crowd points upward and shouts, "The Emperor is wearing no clothes." A great hush moves through the crowd as the townspeople awaken to the truth. Through the innocent eyes of a child the greed and folly of the king is revealed.

Questions

As I embody my ability to create abundance and power in the world, what new foundation am I building within my life?

Am I awake and willing to examine the truth of world affairs and political agendas, even if my questioning prompts me to look into my own use of power, monetary security, and comfort?

What does true authority look like to me?

Affirmations

My ability to discern the difference between the illusion of power and true empowerment has become keen and integral.

I detach myself from the vale of illusions that haunts the material world.

V
THE WIZARD:
THE HIEROPHANT

The Wizard

"Suddenly he was aware of himself again. Frodo, neither the Voice nor the Eye: free to choose, and with one remaining instant in which to do so. He took the Ring off his finger. He was kneeling in clear sunlight before the high seat. A black shadow seemed to pass like an arm above him; it missed Amon Hen and groped out west, and faded. Then all the sky was clean and blue and birds sang in every tree."
—J.R.R. Tolkien,
The Fellowship of the Ring

Traditional Meaning

There have been two primary figures represented in this card over the centuries. Originally, it was a clear picture of the Pope, the ultimate father figure, rather stern and somber in bearing, as the leader of the Catholic Church and religion. He sits on a throne (like the traditional images of The Empress and The Emperor) with two priests kneeling before him and the crossed keys that symbolize heaven and earth, or sometimes heaven and hell. As the tarot evolved, this paternal figure shifted into a more comfortable form—that of a Hierophant, a teacher of ageless wisdom, a guide into higher realms of consciousness, someone more compatible with Trump number II, The High Priestess. This card is associated with the zodiacal sign Taurus. Some researchers point to the importance of the sense of hearing when this card is present. The fine art of listening to the still, small voice within is crucial when the Hierophant makes an appearance. While it may seem that this unusual mentor is external in your life, perhaps it represents the accumulated knowledge you have gained over many lifetimes. As such, this initiator into the secret mysteries of life is really a harbinger of your own expertise and eternal wisdom.

Keywords

Ethics; conformity; tradition; intuition; revelation; assistance; ministry.

Fairy-Tale Lore

There is a combination of excitement and foreboding when we meet up with The Wizard. If the esoteric aphorism is really true—"When the student is ready, the Master appears"—the question is: Are we truly ready for whatever lies ahead? Perhaps there is a simple answer to this question: "Be prepared!" Frodo, as the ring bearer in *The Lord of the Rings* saga, had been prepared spiritually over many lifetimes for his role in the drama. The problem was that he didn't realize it until he actually had to go on the journey, meet his inner and outer demons, and conquer them. That's always part of the story in any fairy tale—you have to ratchet up your determination, courage, and daring to meet any obstacle and, if you do falter from time to time, find a way to pick yourself up and keep trying, even if the odds are stacked against you. This is the cosmic message in the sign of Taurus, still identified with this card. Never give up! Just as the trip undertaken by the fellowship of the ring was going to be arduous and demanded wise use of provisions and personal skills, there is a necessity to consider wise management of your resources whenever this Trump makes an appearance. Cultivate your talent for organization and efficiency. Keep in mind that The Wizard Trump suggests you are going through a spiritual or practical test. Are you being trained for a new job or a higher position within a company or business? If so, your bearing—how you dress, speak, even your body language—will be watched, perhaps by higher-ups, who will be grading your demeanor and considering what future assignments you may safely be given.

Questions

Who are my mentors and teachers guiding me to higher knowledge?
What spiritual discipline will aid my soul-searching quest?
How can I strengthen my bonds to a fellowship, sisterhood, brotherhood, or esoteric order?

Affirmations

In the silence, I hear the inner voice of my higher self.
I am a seeker of the sacred hidden in the material world.

Hansel & Gretel

VI
HANSEL AND GRETEL:
THE LOVERS

"About noon they saw a beautiful bird sitting on a branch of a tree. It sang so sweetly, they stopped to listen. When it finished its song, it spread out its wings, and flew on before them. They followed it until they saw it alight on the roof of a little cottage . . . built entirely of bread, ornamented with cake, and that its windows were of clear sugar."

—"Hansel and Gretel," *Grimm's Fairy Tales,* 1891

Traditional Meaning

Traditionally, The Lovers is a card of decision and responsibility. As Trump number VI, it numerologically stands for loyal devotion to higher principles. One has a choice to follow the well-worn path of desire (the candy cottage in Hansel and Gretel) or stay steady on the path of royal love—where one is not deceived by the enchanting lure of idealized love. The Lovers card suggests we look deeply at the opposing forces in our own hearts and with intelligent foresight and honesty distinguish which path will truly lead to unconditional love. This card denotes a balance between the masculine and the feminine, and in many cases indicates a time in one's life when these two divine principles within must marry. This process would be called the alchemical marriage and this is symbolized by the royal marriage in a fairy tale, when the initiate has merged with both aspects of the divine self. (The princess meets her prince—the feminine has fully merged with the masculine—and thus love and will unite.)

Keywords

Mutual relationship; yearning for harmony; relationship with self and others; higher destiny.

Fairy-Tale Lore

The tale of "Hansel and Gretel" helps us to distinguish the path of true love and devotion from that of fear and desire. We must all find our own way through the vagaries of life and often we come upon the great opportunity to meet the darkened aspects (the witch in the cottage) of our own human nature. We must integrate the feminine principle in a strong and healthy way (Gretel) and save the wounded male within (Hansel who is caged by the enchantress). Hansel and Gretel must find their way back to the original source of love, a hidden treasure that must be earned through the efforts of their devotions to one another and their own wits and intuition. The candy house is only a house of desire, and though it looks like heaven and is sweetly attractive and inviting, it is, in fact, an opportunity for the children to meet the enchantress and to be tested and initiated into a new form of personal mastery. Gretel outsmarts the wicked witch and is able to free Hansel. Together they journey home, each riding separately across the lake upon the back of a beautiful white swan. Although the journey home is a joint effort, each child, the male and the female, must find true strength, individuation, and the ability to cross the shores from one level of consciousness to the next. When they return home, they discover that the mean stepmother (the inner emotion of fear) has died and they are free. True love prevails.

Questions

Have I found a balance within regarding the male and female aspects of my self?

Do I take the time to distinguish between idealized love and romantic fantasy and a mature and masterful understanding of love?
What can I do to master my relationships and bring harmony into them?

Affirmations

I believe that love is unconditional.
I have transformed the illusion of love and purposefully invite the dearest virtue of real love to enter my heart and soul.

Peter Pan

VII
PETER PAN:
THE CHARIOT

"The lovliest tinkle as of golden bells answered him. It is the fairy language. You ordinary children can never hear it, but if you were to hear it, you would know that you had heard it once before."
—J.M. Barrie
Peter and Wendy

Traditional Meaning

The number *seven* signifies movement, domination of spirit over matter, and transitional motion. Therefore, The Chariot represents the psychic mobility that must move inertia and fixation toward creativity where one may retrieve the original gifts of spirit. This is why the card is often referred to as The Journey Home. Passionate ideals and constructive productivity are balanced with this card along with the emotional and intellectual world. The Chariot symbolizes a victorious inner journey where the inner world is filled with creative and inspired visions. The tension of the opposites is released and restored.

Keywords

Balance; mastery; triumph; movement toward a goal; inspired achievements.

Fairy-Tale Lore

In the story of *Peter Pan*, we observe an opportunity to merge the magical with everyday life from the soul's perspective. In many ways this can be a tremendous goal for the initiate who must learn how to balance the world of form and responsibility with spiritual awakening. In *Peter Pan*, Wendy and her brothers are tempted to stay forever in never-never land—or in a state of perpetual bliss—becoming eternal children, never reaching the maturation stage of the human soul. The children symbolize our discovery that we can fly freely within our imagination and dreams. However, we must find our way back to the ground and focus on an ability to integrate the magical with the mundane service and responsibilities we have on earth. When we have taken the time to research the inner realms, traveling to our true home, our origins of magical beauty enable us to fill our lives with wisdom.

Questions

How can I arrange my life so that I can take the time to plug into the spark (Tinkerbell) of my passions and true nature?

I would like to move steadily toward my true inner knowledge and wisdom. What will this journey home look like?

I would like to steer my magical ship home, toward the mastery of self-awareness. What does the Peter Pan archetype mean to me? How does it play out in my life?

Affirmations

My life is a constant journey of exploration, balance, and inspiration.

I am infused with focus and I move forward toward my dreams.

I am journeying home toward the riches of my true self.

Beauty & the Beast

VIII
BEAUTY AND THE BEAST: STRENGTH

"The seeker must be able to hold strict guard over both his thinking and his will. Thereby he becomes in all humility—without presumption—a messenger of the world of the True and Beautiful, and rises to be a participant in the Spirit-World."
—Rudolf Steiner

Traditional Meaning

The Strength card denotes a meeting with our will force and the internal quest for a deeper understanding of power. The traditional image of a woman holding open the mouth of a lion symbolizes the taming of unnatural forces that would induce conflict, aggression, or a wrong use of authority. We learn that there are positive and negative ways to use our natural resources—whether they are personal, of the natural world, or high technology. The Strength card prompts all who reach this phase of growth to tune into the subtle and sublime aspects of power and then, in receptivity, to discover the true power of love.

Keywords

Spiritual, psychic powers; unknown power; power in everyday life; magical helpers.

Fairy-Tale Lore

Beauty and the Beast teaches us many lessons about the power of love and the properties of authentic power and strength. The story opens with an ailing woman (the enchantress) knocking on the door of a castle seeking shelter from the cold. The prince (ego, identity, and will force) rejects her needs and consequently meets the trial of his initiation and awakening (for the ego to see beyond appearances and learn the quality of unconditional love). This represents humanity's blindness to true power and goodness in the material world—also a lesson of Trump number IV, The Emperor's New Clothes. Four plus four equals eight and now we are at the stage of growth when our Emperor aspect has to take the role of an initiate who must obtain greater communication with his higher will if he is to meet life with an open heart. In Beauty and the Beast, we come face to face with the boundaries of the physical plane. Beauty falls in love with the Beast and must face this strange and surreal realization for herself. Her tears of love overflow as she suffers the Beast's imminent death. In fairy-tale lore, the waters of the soul serve as an elixir of healing; Beauty's tears transform the Beast into the handsome prince that he truly is. Now, however, his beauty is genuine, for the enchantress at the beginning of the tale cast the spell of initiation so that he might wake up to a greater understanding of life.

The tale is about transformation. As in many tales, a tower appears, carrying the message of sudden change and transformation. A tower is often discovered at the poignant juncture in a story when a shift is about to occur. In the castle, Beauty finds a tower (transformation) and sees a mirror (coming face to face with what is real), and the mirror says to her, "Through time—in your heart—you will see the truth." And, in time, Beauty sees beyond the outer façade of material form and discovers her deep love for the Beast. This tale offers us all the opportunity to evolve beyond external judgments toward the power of love, above all else.

Questions

How do I examine the world around me?

Do I focus more on the material or do I take time to see beyond external images?

Do I focus on the love of power or the power of love?

Affirmations

I understand that it is love and ONLY pure love that will set me free. The pain of my sorrow is soothed by the endless and infinite love that showers upon me from above.

I am not afraid of my power for I use it according to my higher will.

I can only offer more love and service to the world.

Snow White

IX
SNOW WHITE:
THE HERMIT

"But now the child was all alone in the great forest and she began to run. She ran over sharp stones and through thorns, and the wild beasts ran past her, but did her no harm. She ran as long as her feet would go until it was almost evening: then she saw a little cottage and went into it to rest herself."

—"Snow White,"
Grimm's Fairy Tales, 1891

Traditional Meaning

The Hermit card is a symbolic representation of an inner state of consciousness where one moves to the refuge of solitude and internal healing. This personal journey allows us to gain greater wisdom, teaching us how to use the great jewels of self-knowledge that shine from within the soul. Once the time of internal gestation has been completed, a newfound joy in life is discovered and the liberated self returns to life—refreshed, renewed, and restored.

Keywords

Courage to face oneself; inner knowledge and wisdom; retreat; service.

Fairy-Tale Lore

Snow White's mother has died and fate has offered her a mean and jealous stepmother (representing chaos and transformation) who banishes her to the woods (The Hermit) to be killed by the huntsman

97

(our mortal conscious mind). Goodness prevails and Snow White (the divine quest for purity and truth) is set free by the huntsman to fend for herself in the deep, dark woods where she discovers her place of retreat and transformation, the dwarves' cottage.

The little dwarves who work in the underground jewel mines represent Snow White's need to move into the caverns of her own darkened world and retrieve the true riches that lie beneath the surface. As they unearth and offer Snow White riches, they become her spiritual helpers and serve as the guiding lights that assist Snow White as she discovers her path toward empowerment.

However, the dwarves are unable to dislodge the piece of poisoned apple from Snow White's throat. This is the task her own soul must complete, for her throat represents the fifth chakra, the area of the body where we speak and express our truth. Snow White must remain in her crystal coffin until her prince (her higher will) finds her and awakens her to a new life.

Questions

What precious space or retreat can I create for myself so that I may take the time to unite with my inner wisdom and truth?

During this time of inward reflection, what parts of myself would be most beneficial to explore and unite with?

What new level of service am I being asked to explore?

Affirmations

I enter the deep caverns of my soul.
I find the treasures that make me whole.

X

ALICE IN WONDERLAND: THE WHEEL OF FORTUNE

Alice in Wonderland

"How puzzling all these changes are! I'm never sure what I'm going to be, from one minute to another! However, I've got back to my right size: the next thing is, to get into that beautiful garden—how is that to be done I wonder?"

—Lewis Carroll, *Alice in Wonderland*

Traditional Meaning

If we consider The Fool (0) and The World (XXI) to be intrinsically and cyclically linked as the Alpha (start) and Omega (end) of the higher journey through life, death, and rebirth, then that leaves twenty Major Trumps. The halfway point, the center, is The Wheel of Fortune. In traditional images, this wheel often has four Hebrew letters—T, A, R, O—representing the Tetragrammaton, the four-lettered name of Jehovah, the God of the Israelites. The four letters also connect to the four cardinal points of the compass and year, and various cryptic alchemical symbols. Usually overlighted by a Sphinx (representing the mystery of what it is to be truly human) and appearing in the clouds, the wheel is suspended in space while in the four corners of this card are revealed the celestial images of the four fixed power signs of the zodiac (the Bull for Taurus; the Lion for Leo; the Eagle for Scorpio; and the Angel or Human Being for Aquarius). The card itself is connected to Jupiter (the greater benefic in astrology) and suggests that something fortuitous, positive, and life-enhancing is on the verge of happening. However, on a deeper level, this is a Trump card of both ups *and* downs, a wheel not only of gains but of karma (expressing the law of cause and effect, reaping what you have sown). Just because a golden opportunity appears on the horizon doesn't mean you will have the capacity to seize hold of it. Much will depend on everything you have learned thus far on your life path. The key to The Wheel of Fortune is in the word *centering*.

Keywords

Center; destiny; fortune; karma; opportunity; cyclical change; turning around; cause and effect.

Fairy-Tale Lore

As explained in the original book accompanying the *Inner Child Cards* deck, Alice in Wonderland has much to do with "right timing." The White Rabbit, one of the central characters, keeps pulling out a pocket watch, saying "I'm late for an important date." Alice is clearly on a fantastic journey—of the mind, imagination, and spirit. She's entered the kaleidoscopic realm of dreams and visions, we might even say the province of the collective unconscious of humanity where mythology and fairy-tale lore have their true origin. It's easy to get mentally confused, emotionally drained, and spiritually bewildered when one is floating in the midst of myriad images, archetypes, and principles of higher law. To cope with this phantasmagoria, you need to pause, center yourself, and raise your consciousness to a more exalted plane. Perhaps a meditation technique, type of yoga, or tai chi exercise will help you do this. Like the whirling dervishes of ancient Persia, even learning a new dance may assist you in coming to grips with the dizzying array of ideas streaming into your head.

An essential truth within this Trump is guiding you to learn to be in the right place, at the right time, and in the right state of consciousness. When this trinity takes hold—aligning space, time, and clear thinking—you will be blessed with some kind of fortune or abundance offered by the celestial provider, Jupiter. The warning in this card is to beware of over-indulgence, over-optimism, and too much of a good thing. Just as Alice is inundated with a multitude of experiences, if your life is too full of plans, dates, and activities, you won't accomplish your most significant goals with finesse. You will become lost in wonderland. As with the traditional Trump, this card reminds you to find a way to the central core of your being, not letting the spinning fancies of the mind or the variety of external enticements lead you away from what beats within your heart.

Questions

Am I spinning out of control in my main work and life direction?
Can my greatest dreams be realized in physical expression?
What imaginative gifts can I summon to create a continuing flow of abundance in my life?

Affirmations

I am wealthy in physical, emotional, mental, and spiritual riches.
My imagination is an overflowing fount of divine wisdom.

XI
THE MIDAS TOUCH: JUSTICE

The Midas Touch

"In order to give a solid direction to one's life and to estimate correctly one's actions and their consequences, one has to allow the largely ignored aspirations and urges of the unconscious to challenge self-satisfaction with one's successful conscious choices."

—Dr. Irene Gad,
Tarot and Individuation

Traditional Meaning

In the traditional tarot card, Justice, we see a woman seated upon a mighty throne that is sturdy and secure. She holds a long sword in her right hand, for she must enforce decisions and judgments with the clarity of clear-mindedness. (The sword represents clarity, focus, and mental skill.) This card greets us at a time in life when we must establish order and justice within our inner being. An individual must create order within his or her own heart and soul and face the direction that will set things right. One must create balance in everyday life. We learn to discern and observe the laws of the higher world from an objective perspective. This card represents the scales or wheel of fate and the Tree of Life. What goes up, must come down.

Keywords

Balance; oscillation between opposites; karma; equality; truth; human justice and cosmic justice.

Fairy-Tale Lore

King Midas balanced his accounts each day, stacking his gold and his wealth against the values of his life. His attachments to the material world outweighed his understanding of the law of cosmic justice and spiritual insight, of the need to "balance one's accounts" and be weighed in the celestial scales as a human soul. Therefore, when he wished that all that he touched would turn to gold, he became cursed by the enchantress who granted his wish. He was given a tragic life lesson through his own desire and greed. First, when he turned the beautiful roses in the garden to gold, he brought great sadness to his beloved daughter who loved the fragrant flowers of the earth. As he reached to comfort her, he turned his own dear daughter to gold. Alone with all of his gold and wealth, the King was full of sorrow and wished that all could return as it was before his golden wish. In order for King Midas to clear the spell, he was instructed by the enchantress to dive into a pool of water with a special vase and pour water on everything that he had turned to gold. The water represents the return to the divine waters of the feminine, where the feeling world touches the heart and balances the arid confines of old mental constructs. When the feeling and the thinking worlds are brought to balance, it is only then that justice rewards those who see and act in a balanced way.

Questions

What is out of balance in my life?

If I were to look carefully into myself, what must I do to set things in karmic order and balance?

Do I appreciate all that I am granted?

Am I grateful for my life as it is?

If I wish for more, is that in balance with the laws of cosmic justice and balance?

Affirmations

I take responsibility for all of my actions.

I walk my talk.

I understand the great wheel of fate and, with this keen insight, I choose a higher understanding of life's consequences and offerings.

Life is my mirror.

XII
JACK AND THE BEANSTALK: THE HANGED ONE

Jack & the Beanstalk

"Things are very different in 'Jack and the Beanstalk.' This story tells that while belief in magic can help in daring to meet the world on our own, in the last analysis we must take the initiative and be willing to run the risks involved in mastering life. When Jack is given the magic seeds, he climbs the beanstalk on his own initiative, not because somebody suggested it."

—Bruno Bettelheim,
The Uses of Enchantment

Traditional Meaning

In traditional imagery, we see a man, perhaps the suspended Magician, willingly and quite happily hanging upside down from the Tree of Life. He has reversed his position in order to gain a new perspective on life, to surrender the old ways to a higher calling, to put an ear to the earth, so to speak, and listen to the intuitive message of Mother Earth (his high self). Symbolically, when receiving this card in a session, one has emptied out the pockets of the past and is learning, through the will of the high self, to be perceptive of what is yet to come. Most importantly, it must be noted that the individual is choosing this new position in life and is learning the true meaning of sacrifice, which is "to make life sacred."

Keywords

Timeless space; patient waiting; tapping the layers of the unconscious; sacrifice of ego for the higher good.

Fairy-Tale Lore

In the tale of "Jack and the Beanstalk," it did not seem an intelligent decision for Jack to exchange the family cow for three magical seeds. However, if we ignore the logic and the rational reality (the planet Neptune rules the Hanged One or Jack in the Beanstalk) and open to the unseen miracles of life's journey, then we can understand why Jack chose to receive the three seeds from the stranger. In fairy-tale lore, many tests and initiations are offered in the power of three. Jack is offered a test from the Queen of Heaven (The Empress is Trump number III) to see if he could surrender himself to a higher destiny. Attachment to earthly resolutions could only further the family's poverty. Jack reversed his logic and united with his higher imagination. His mother's angry despair as she tosses the beans out the window represents our earthly fear and the material attachments that can blind us from cosmic timing and miracle. In the night, representing the dream-weaving time of the unconscious, a giant stalk has grown, representing the umbilical cord between heaven and earth. This cord becomes the conduit by which Jack may retrieve the original treasures of his own soul, his father's riches, and the chance to start life anew. This gift is granted due to the fact that Jack surrendered to the conditions of his life. He trusted the changes that were fated to take place due to the agreement to trade the family cow—the material world and attachments—for three magical seeds representing the potential for new growth and abundance.

Questions

What am I being asked to surrender or let go of?
Am I overly attached to my material world?
Do I trust in the process of letting go?

Affirmations

I am attuned to my higher will.
I am willing and able to let go of the rational and logical attachments of my everyday life so that I may surrender to the unknown future with ease and comfort.

XIII
SLEEPING BEAUTY: DEATH

Sleeping Beauty

"The hundred years had passed, and the day arrived when Briar Rose would be awakened from her sleep. As the prince approached the hedge, instead of thorns and briars, he saw only flowers."

—"Sleeping Beauty,"
Grimm's Fairy Tales, 1891

Traditional Meaning

The Death card symbolizes the parts of our lives that must change. Old forms of consciousness must die in order for the birth of the new to emerge. Themes that are included in this card are rites of passage, death and rebirth issues, and rituals that involve letting go of the past; it can occasionally indicate an actual death in the material world. The card implies transformation at the deepest level. One may no longer hold on to the old patterns that once dictated daily life.

Changes appear to us in many ways. It is significant that, in the previous Major card, The Hanged One shows us the inverted Death. Death brings new life. We are brought to the fire of the spirit which will restore the faith of the soul.

Keywords

Change; transformation; transition; renewed beginnings after a catharsis.

Fairy-Tale Lore

The enchanting birth of little Briar Rose created such excitement that the King decided to hold a great banquet to which all of the wise women of the land would be invited. However, he had only twelve golden plates, so only twelve of the thirteen wise women were invited. Thirteen is the number of the Death card and so here we see a very profound correlation with the "Briar Rose" or "Sleeping Beauty" fable. The uninvited thirteenth fairy or wise woman was the enchantress who cast the spell on the baby girl that in her fifteenth year she would prick her finger and fall dead. The twelfth fairy—Trump number XII is The Hanged One in traditional tarot—tempered the curse which then fated the child to one hundred years of sleep instead of death.

The Death card often appears for young people during the time of adolescence or at the beginning of menstrual cycles, or for women at the onset of menopause. There are fated changes and new states of consciousness that will inevitably come into a person's life. Even though we may wish to avoid these changes or life cycles, we must meet them and allow the transformations to occur. Age fifteen signals the time of life when we meet our shadow (represented by The Big Bad Wolf or The Devil card) and peek into the unknown parts of our psyche. At age fifteen Briar Rose finds herself alone in the castle to wander at will. When she comes to an old tower, she follows a narrow winding stairway upward until she comes to a little door. This door is the passage she must venture through in order to complete the karmic imprint of her soul, falling asleep for one hundred years until her higher self, represented by the prince, enchants her with a kiss of awakening.

Questions

What passage awaits me at this time?

A deep transformation awaits me. What must I let go of?

What door must I walk through in order that I may meet the next stage of my life?

Affirmations

The changes in my life offer me the opportunities I need to re-awaken the deepest destiny I hold.

XIV

THE GUARDIAN ANGEL: TEMPERANCE

The Guardian Angel

"Angel of God,
My Guardian Dear,
To Whom God's love commits me here,
Ever this day be at my side,
To Light and Guard,
To Rule and Guide."

—Prayer to the Guardian Angel

Traditional Meaning

In the traditional Temperance card, a woman measures out and weighs something. This card represents a superior consciousness that links to her sacred wisdom. In *Inner Child Cards*, we see a boy and girl, representing the higher mind and the higher heart. The tension between the sources of the positive and negative poles is life itself. These energies—yin and yang, day and night, heaven and earth—bestow life on everything that lives in creation. After the transformation of Trump number XIII, the ego is in the process of reuniting with the self. Temperance denotes balance, renewal of ideas, purification, and confirmation.

Keywords

The art of balance; grounding cosmic wisdom; art; focus; careful expansion.

Fairy-Tale Lore

In ancient myth angels are said to be the very breath of God—the messengers of love, light, and wisdom. All human beings are blessed with angelic helpers and guides who nurture them and protect them along the way. They are the bridges to the heavenly worlds and they wrap their love around us and remind us that we are not without the guidance and protection of the spiritual world. In fairy tales and fables, the helpful Guardian Angel may be depicted as a fairy, helpful elves, wizards, birds of many kinds, or other animals and plants of the natural world.

When you are feeling out of balance—be it emotionally, physically, mentally, or spiritually—remember to call upon that which you are neglecting in your life. Ask for the guidance and help that is surrounding you. Take time in your day to ground whatever chaotic energy has caused you to become uncentered. In times of crisis, we are called upon to "alter our life." Perhaps it will serve you to create an altar or spiritual space in your home that will serve as a healing reminder that you are blessed.

Questions

What can I do in my life that will help me balance my everyday life with the virtues of my spiritual needs?

What measures can I take that will help me to ground the insights and visions I carry in my soul in my practical life?

How may I move beyond the polarities that split my perception of wholeness?

Affirmations

I walk my path in life holding the balance of my spiritual and physical worlds within my heart.

My Guardian Angel blesses and protects me each and every day.

The Big Bad Wolf

XV
THE BIG BAD WOLF:
THE DEVIL

"It is not so coincidental that wolves and coyotes, bears and wildish women have similar reputations. They all share related, instinctual archetypes and, as such, both are erroneously reputed to be ungracious, wholly, and innately dangerous and ravenous."
—Clarissa Pinkola Estes,
Women Who Run with the Wolves

Traditional Meaning

In the traditional tarot, Trump number XV, The Devil, is associated with the law of matter, of manifestation in solid or material form. If this energy remains unconscious as it manifests in the human being, it can become stagnant, unyielding, and resistant. Human beings must learn to balance the power of the material realm with the law of spirituality and higher consciousness. When the spirit is denied, one must meet the shadow of the soul where fears, attachments, and rigid patterns prevail. A meeting with this shadow aspect of the psyche will surely challenge a person to experience liberation from the past and be reborn to a new consciousness and freedom.

Keywords

Testing; consequences of unconscious; negative contents within the soul; limitations; inertia; resistance; fear.

Fairy-Tale Lore

When we meet The Big Bad Wolf, we come face to face with our wild nature or the untamed aspects of our personality. That the Wolf is called "bad" signifies the way in which we (the collective) fear our shadow and the power of the dark world. Fairy tales offer a rich and fertile ground where one may explore the lurking depths of unconscious debris that has been submerged since childhood, perhaps even from past lives. These opportunities come in the guise of dark enchantresses, wicked stepmothers, dragons, beasts, and lost journeys through the thick and darkened woods. Through these characters and experiences we come into direct contact with the fractured aspects of the emotional and mental realm.

When Little Red Cap meets The Big Bad Wolf, she is symbolically meeting the force that will internally liberate her from innocent folly. What might she gain and what might she lose? There is always a mixed dilemma in our search for consciousness, for once we become awake we have a responsibility to remain on a path of truth and wisdom. If we fail to learn our lessons and to grow beyond the folly of youth—a path that will inevitably be seasoned with the mistakes and actions that serve as the stepping-stones to a richer and more responsible life—we will come closer to meeting The Big Bad Wolf in our own backyard.

Questions

What areas of my life do I block due to fear, anger, or issues of the past that I am unable to heal?

What actions would I need to take in order to move forward?

What would be the benefit of such action?

Affirmations

I am ready and willing to move beyond the crystallization of my fears. As I walk forward, untethering myself from the bondage of my past, I am radiant and full of light.

I will not look back.

XVI
RAPUNZEL: THE TOWER

Rapunzel

"Rapunzel grew to be the most beautiful child under the sun. When she was twelve years old, the witch locked her in a tower in the forest. The tower had neither steps nor doors, only a little window at the top."
—"Rapunzel,"
Grimm's Fairy Tales, 1891

Traditional Meaning

The traditional Tower card shows lightning striking the top of the structure, symbolizing a sudden and natural change in a person's life. Of whatever was in place prior to the evolutionary step of meeting The Tower, nothing will or can remain the same. When The Tower strikes, the individual needs to find refuge and solace within the sanctuary of aloneness and solitude to fully digest the transformation to newfound values and identity. These changes are precipitated by circumstances beyond an individual's power, arising from within or without. In any case, The Tower shifts the structure of the old and ruthlessly shatters the security of the past. One must move forward.

Keywords

Awakening; redemption; transformation; sudden change; surprise.

Fairy-Tale Lore

The Tower is a powerful metaphor of transformation in fairy-tale literature. In the tale of "Briar Rose" or "Sleeping Beauty," it is the enchanted curse that ushers Briar Rose into the tower and up the wooden stairs to the room where she discovers the irresistible spindle that pricks her finger. In the tale of "Beauty and the Beast," Beauty discovers the magic mirror that tells of her destiny in a tower. In "Rapunzel," the tower represents the enchantment stage where Rapunzel must undergo the shift to young womanhood. At age twelve (Trump number XII is that of The Hanged One or Jack and the Beanstalk, which denotes a time when one's world is turned upside down), she is locked in the tower. There she unites with her own sexuality and desire for new freedom. All of these tales offer the potent symbol of the tower as a means of transforming the fate of the character, leading her to the final stage of awakening.

Sudden and unexpected events dictate the fate of Rapunzel throughout the fable. Her father gathers lettuce from a garden belonging to an enchantress in order to nurture his pregnant wife. He visits the garden three times (again the magic of the number *three*); the third time he is discovered by the enchantress and cursed by her magic spell. As often happens in fairy-tale lore, a baby is fated to meet the task of individuation. Eventually Rapunzel, her long braid cut by the revengeful enchantress, is cast away to the desert where in exile she must summon her will force and call her blinded prince back to her. Once her tears restore the sight of her prince, Rapunzel is free, whole, and ready to engage with the destiny of a new life.

Questions

What areas in my life are in the greatest need of change and awakening?
How does the tower of transformation summon me to let go of the past and purge the old?
What new steps of empowerment must I take?

Affirmations

My life is in constant rhythm of change and growth.
I feel safe amid these transformations for I am ready to meet the new life that awaits me.

Wishing Upon a Star

XVII
WISHING UPON A STAR: THE STAR

"Just as evening gives birth to morning, so from the darkness arises a new light; the Stella Matutina, which is at once the evening and the morning star."

—Carl Jung,
as quoted in Irene Gad,
Tarot and Individuation

Traditional Meaning

The Star card implies that the individual on the Royal Road to Wisdom has now unveiled the essential qualities of cosmic consciousness. The beautiful, naked woman in the traditional version has one foot on the land (the conscious realm) and the other in the water (the unconscious realm). Similarly, The Wishing Upon A Star card reveals the young lad with one foot on land and the other reaching toward the well—the deep waters of the soul. This card denotes a positive outpouring of good intention. The flower of the soul is fully opened and is conscious of this beautiful initiation where wishes and dreams prompt the soul to share the virtues of cosmic riches with others. One's truest and highest wish would be to participate in the great work of the world and become like a shining star in the dark sky.

Keywords

Meditation; inner light; spiritual perception; hope; wishes.

Fairy-Tale Lore

The Star represents the beginning of true initiation. The darkened night is sequenced with an array of brilliant lights, all of which shine upon the dreaming of humanity. As we sleep and dream, our unconscious self is stirred by the dynamic language of the inner landscape of personal perceptions and experiences. The Star offers us conscious awareness that there is great light within each human soul and that each human spirit is always able to ascend to this greater knowledge. As I was writing this chapter at the coast in Oregon, I walked into a little store to purchase a gift for a friend when, out of the blue, the friendly store clerk offered me this quote: "The only way to make sure your dreams will come true is to wake up." She didn't know how very perfect her timing was to share her lovely words with me. The Star card is magic.

Questions

This is a time of awakening and inspiration. How can I open my heart to this blessed time of initiation and growth?

The mystic's soul is guided by the stars, inspired by the heart, and when opened to the heavenly influences, reaches toward enlightenment. How may this radiant light guide me toward my highest dreams?

Affirmations

My inner vision is like a flowering rose blossoming toward awareness. I go to the waters of my deepest wishes and ask that they may come true. The twinkling stars are a mirror to the joy and wonder that inspire me each day.

Cinderella

XVIII
CINDERELLA:
THE MOON

"So it was Cinderella's father who brought her the twig from the Hazel bush. She thanked him for it, and went out immediately and planted it on her mother's grave. Poor little Cinderella wept bitterly, and her tears fell on the twig and watered it. In a little while it grew to a beautiful tree, and here she would come three times a day and pray and weep."
—"Cinderella,"
Grimm's Fairy Tales, 1891

Traditional Meaning

In the traditional tarot, Trump XVIII is The Moon. Traditional imagery shows a large lunar disc containing the face of a beautiful woman. It indicates the activity of the spirit, foresight, and individual regeneration through awareness of the feeling-world, the emotions, which sometimes are an aspect of the shadow self. The Moon represents our emotional patterns and needs, our sensitivity, and past. It symbolizes the inner feminine, influencing the relationships and nurturance that we cultivate.

Keywords

Expansion of consciousness; abandonment issues; instinctual forces; the watery and ever-changing emotions and feelings of an individual; karmic past.

Fairy-Tale Lore

The story of Cinderella teaches us about the virtues of service as a means toward initiation. At the beginning of the story, Cinderella shows us that we must water our life with faith and the acceptance of our loss and sorrow. The hazelnut branch that her father offers her is buried at the grave of her deceased mother. Each day, as she weeps over the branch, her tears moisten the earth, enabling the branch to grow into a beautiful Tree of Life that will attract all the birds of the heavens. The birds, an aspect of the Holy Mother, assist her with the tasks of the wicked stepmother. In the old Grimm version, the original Fairy Godmother is represented by the birds in the heavenly tree; these birds represent Cinderella's spiritual forces at work.

Cinderella is archetypally connected to The Moon because she, like many other fairy-tale heroines, is cut from the umbilical cord of the past at the beginning of the story. This enables her to be free of the past and to heal its karmic imprints. Her stepsisters are still very much attached to the material world, and have not been given the liberty to move through the passages of transformation yet. They are part of the darkened force within the tale along with the stepmother. They provide the fertile ground where Cinderella must meet her tasks and initiation.

Cinderella's greatest gift is her compassion and understanding. The Moon card is ruled by the zodiacal sign of Pisces, which in turn rules the feet. As Cinderella goes through her stages of evolution, her feet—that which she stands upon and, therefore, another virtue of understanding—are emphasized by the different shoes that she wears in the tale. When she is still in her sorrow, moving through her karmic past, she wears little wooden shoes. She is still of the earth plane and has not reached spiritual maturation. Later in the tale, she wears glass shoes or, in the old Grimm tale, shoes of crystal. As Cinderella refines her understanding, she grows more and more loving and responsive to her new life.

Questions

Do I take the time to water the Tree of My Own Life?

Am I in touch with my true needs and emotions?

What are the karmic imprints that have offered me the greatest gift of initiation and growth in this lifetime?

Do I allow my own spiritual guides to assist me as I move through the challenges and tests of my soul?

Affirmations

I understand that the true meaning of sacrifice is "to make life sacred."

My life is sacred as I meet the tasks and work of my life destiny.

I am at peace with my internal and external image of "mother."

As I honor my truest needs, the universe shall shower me with eternal reward.

Through my tears, my soul shall be moistened and my fertile inner life will be fed, honored, and nurtured.

XIX
THE YELLOW BRICK ROAD: THE SUN

The Yellow Brick Road

"There were several roads near by, but it did not take her long to find the one paved with yellow brick. Within a short time she was walking briskly toward the Emerald City, her silver shoes tinkling merrily on the hard, yellow roadbed. The sun shone bright and the birds sang sweetly, and Dorothy did not feel nearly so bad as you might think a little girl would who had been suddenly whisked away from her own country and set down in the midst of a strange land."

—Lyman Frank Baum, *The Wizard of Oz*

Traditional Meaning

The Sun card represents active and conscious participation in life, and the joy and celebration it can stir within the soul. When The Sun's rays penetrate the earth, our eyes rejoice in the colors of nature and the path we walk upon is readily visible. This is an expanded energy, one of open-ended possibilities and goals. Ruled by Leo, The Sun is a mirror to the ego consciousness of an individual and often represents a time of growth and new identity or rebirth. The self must go through many initiations and cycles, and The Sun card appears when one is radiant with the light of healing and life-renewing inspirations.

Keywords

Unity of life; joy; enthusiasm; fulfillment; fertility; creative inspiration.

Fairy-Tale Lore

Most of us are familiar with the story of *The Wizard of Oz*. The golden brick road that Dorothy and her friends traveled on is one of the best-known aspects of the story. "Follow the Yellow Brick Road" has become a metaphor for life's many adventures and expeditions. When we hear the quote, it often conjures up thoughts of hopes, dreams, ambitions, and trust. Dorothy is lost and quite frightened until she finds herself sure-footed and hopeful upon the yellow bricks of the winding path toward the Emerald City, for she has become conscious of what she must do to get back home. Just as the Sun guides us in the bright daylight, so, too, the Yellow Brick Road was the outer journey that led Dorothy to her friends and guides—the Straw Man, the Tin Man, and the Lion. Let us not forget Toto, who, in a whimsical way, represents the dog who barks at the heels of The Fool in the traditional tarot. Now that Dorothy is well on her way toward higher consciousness, the little dog has become a companion and a true ally on the path toward future ambitions and prospects. Animals and the different ways they appear in tarot cards, myths, and fairy tales represent the various stages of the will and primal instincts within the human psyche. As a companion and ally, Toto represents the unity of the will and the heart. Toto is loyal and protective toward Dorothy; thus her own will is in harmony with her heart. On the journey of the Yellow Brick Road, Dorothy and her fellow companions are all seeking unity and wholeness. Each one needs some vital part of themselves validated; thus, this is the path of the higher ego. The Sun, as the Yellow Brick Road, denotes this wonderful quest.

Questions

On the winding path of life, what are my truest goals and ambitions?
If I look objectively at my life, what main trait or attribute am I seeking union with?
What brings me the greatest joy in life?

Affirmations

I am a radiant light of hope, love, and inspiration.
I walk purposefully and joyfully toward my higher ambitions.
I am conscious and fully awake. I walk forward into a new day of hope and love.

The Three Little Pigs

XX
THE THREE LITTLE PIGS: JUDGMENT

"Who's afraid of the Big Bad Wolf,
The Big Bad Wolf,
The Big Bad Wolf,
Who's afraid of The Big Bad Wolf . . ."
—"The Three Little Pigs"

Traditional Meaning

In the Judgment card we must face our actions, judgments, and that which keeps us from moving onward to where healing and forgiveness are found. The resurrection into purification and release is possible now; the seeker on the path to rebirth is ready to find a way to master life by confronting the shadows that led him or her toward fear and defeat. In many instances this is a card of healing and a joyous celebration into maturation.

Keywords

Instant realization; purification; healing judgment; forgiveness.

Fairy-Tale Lore

The story of "The Three Little Pigs" is a well-loved nursery rhyme for it plainly spells out the fate of one who is lazy or irresponsible and the consequences that might befall him or her. We must all eventually wake up to the rebirth of a heightened vision. We have the opportunity to learn by our mistakes, for many of us will build a house (our spiritual foundation) out of weakened materials (half-hearted devotion and focus) like the first and second little pigs who played all day and built their houses of straw and twigs. However, the third little pig works hard day and night to build a sturdy house of bricks. The cunning wolf is able to outsmart the first and second little pigs (the shadow self can easily destroy that which is not firmly established in the development of self-mastery).

In his book *The Uses of Enchantment*, Bruno Bettelheim refers to the fable as a lesson in the Pleasure Principle versus the Reality Principle. He states: "The Three Little Pigs teaches the child in a most enjoyable and dramatic form that we must not be lazy and take things easy, for if we do, we may perish. Intelligent planning and foresight combined with hard labor will make us victorious over even our most ferocious enemy—The Wolf."*

The third little pig demonstrates being non-judgmental as he offers his frivolous brothers protection from the perils of the wolf and their own folly. In the end, the wolf falls down the chimney into the boiling soup and is transformed.

Questions

If I take charge of my life with earnest focus and joy, what changes may I come upon?

In what areas might I use wise discretion so that I may build a strong and safe foundation for my healing and spiritual grounding?

*Bettelheim, *The Uses of Enchantment*, 42.

Affirmations

The judgments in my life have turned into observations that can guide and assist me in understanding my life without the destructive qualities of self-criticism and shame.

I am in the process of healing judgments in my life.

I release the judgments from my past.

My focus is on healing and forgiving.

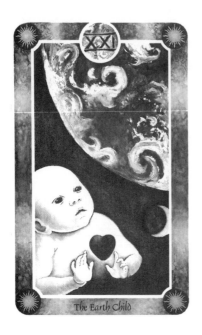

The Earth Child

XXI
THE EARTH CHILD: THE WORLD

"Come to this life like a warrior,
Nothing will bore you,
You can be happy,
Let in the light, it will heal you,
And you can feel you,
To sing out a Song of the Soul."
—Cris Williamson,
Song of the Soul

Traditional Meaning

In the traditional tarot card of The World, a beautiful dancing woman is depicted at the center, surrounded by the four fixed zodiacal signs of Taurus, Leo, Scorpio, and Aquarius. This card represents arrival at a universal and cosmic apex where freedom and form have won their way to balanced mastery within the individual. The World card heralds the Queen of Heaven and Earth, representing skill and productivity. She is the Universal Mother and her dance represents the rhythms of nature and the cycles of life, death, and rebirth.

Keywords

Cosmic consciousness; enlightenment; eternal meaning; graceful and skilled responsibilities.

Fairy-Tale Lore

The Earth Child card allows the individual another glimpse of the power of the eternal and divine feminine consciousness. It shows the image of the Holy Child who has birthed itself within the consciousness of humanity. The beautiful baby (male or female) is a pure representation of the Holy Mother's gift, the pure incarnate treasure birthed from the holy vessel of divine consciousness. The emblem of the heart reveals the love principle that has been born out of the Moon. (The Moon in the foreground is a crescent, symbolizing new beginnings and action.) One has been invited to enter the realm of cosmic consciousness to prepare for an opportunity to serve the world with a pure heart and an open mind.

Questions

The Earth Child offers me a glimpse of the skills and opportunities that I must accept. What are these talents and how may I perfect this opportunity?

How do I define freedom in my life?

Do I stifle it by focusing on limiting thought forms?

In what way might I bring this joyous rebirth to the events of my everyday life?

Affirmations

I am a beautiful child of worth and the world offers me full participation and acceptance.

I have a solid foundation from which to stand and serve the world.

Chapter 9

The Minor Arcana

The Minor Arcana is broken down into four suits representing the four elements of fire, earth, air, and water. Over the centuries, the suit names have often changed to reflect the paradigms and values of the culture. For example, the ancient name for the currently accepted designation in tarot decks of "pentacles" was "coins." Some tarot creators have also used the name of "disks" for this suit. Within *Inner Child Cards*, this suit is now called "Earth Crystals." In another example, what we refer to as "Magic Wands" were once called "Wands" and for many centuries were named "rods." Our suit names reflect the intrinsic nature of the spirit pervading *Inner Child Cards*. Each suit consists of ten numerical cards and four court cards. These cards are more personal than the Major Arcana cards. The numerical cards represent the practical encounters that one has each day and the court cards represent the picture or energy field of the individual or of the people and circumstances involved in his or her daily encounters. This section of the book offers an expanded explanation of each card and serves as additional information to accompany the material within the *Inner Child Cards* book and deck set. Each card's description is divided into three categories as follows:

Traditional Meaning: This offers a framework of information that sketches an idea of the meaning of each card throughout history. It is helpful to have this background information to help formulate a more complete understanding of the holistic meaning and symbolism for each card.

Inner Child Cards: This explanation provides a deeper understanding of the message each *Inner Child Card* has to offer. Connecting this definition with the traditional meaning gives a well-worn meaning a new twist or angle. Open your heart and mind to the healing and teaching contained in this section.

Questions: You might like to answer the questions offered in this section by writing them down in a journal or hold the thoughts and inquiries in your own mind and meditate on them. These questions are offered as food for thought and will hopefully aid in the process of digesting the meaning of each card.

The Magic Wands

Ace of Wands

ACE OF WANDS

Traditional Meaning

This card shows the energies that arise after blocks and old patterns have been resolved. Often depicted as a bolt of fire or light, the Ace of Wands transforms and revitalizes that which has been stagnant. It is said to be the second highest energy card in the deck after The Sun. This card stimulates the intuition, creative endeavors, sexuality, kundalini, and the drives that move a person toward awakened consciousness.

Inner Child Cards

The Ace of Wands is depicted as a vibrant butterfly magnifying the potential for rebirth and vibrant creativity. This magical occurrence is assisted by the whimsical flower fairies adorned with fiery red hair who are unwrapping the potential of this new life force. This is a magic wand—a source of inspiration and light. Its radiant source is available now. Use it to your fullest potential.

Questions

How can I fully engage in this vibrant energy that has embraced my life?

How can I best embody and digest these new potentials in order that I may balance them in my daily life?

What new parts of myself are awakening?

TWO OF WANDS

Traditional Meaning

In traditional decks, the Two of Wands represents the positive union between the dynamic interplay of the inner domain of the psyche and the way in which one is guided by its intuitive creativity in everyday life. The card suggests that an individual seek to establish a harmonious union with the principles of inspiration and application. There is the potential to balance the fiery surge of new insight with well-grounded instincts.

Inner Child Cards

The Two of Magic Wands pictures a beautiful and contemplative flower fairy who is looking deeply into the waters of her own inner reflection. Her body, ablaze with light, unifies with the watery depths of the unconscious. She has a real view of the deeper picture of her true face, which is adorned with a wreath of flowers that creates a bountiful aura around her crown chakra. All objects in the picture have a divine mirroring and reflective quality. One may ponder and quest for the true reality that represents life. The Two of Magic Wands is a kind of looking glass of the soul where we come face to face with a need to unify and identify the mystical qualities of future prospects with vision and clarity.

Questions

Do I trust my inner visions and do I listen to the subtle promptings of my intuitive guidance?

Am I centered and in harmony with my creative gift of spiritual insight? How can I offer this gift to the world?

Three of Wands

THREE OF WANDS

Traditional Meaning

This card denotes an awakening to the joys of virtue, self-confidence, and integrity regarding one's creative and innovative passions. The wisdom within this card counteracts doubt and worry within the soul. The number *three*, connected to the vital, fiery potential of the Wand suit, carries goodwill and bestows great self-confidence and empowerment on the individual. One is unable to attach to the rigid confines of the intellect for the number *three* implies a sensual connection to nature. The Wands enlighten the mind to higher states of understanding, which include imagination and intuitive perspectives.

Inner Child Cards

Music is a language of the soul that extends beyond the boundaries of the rational mind. The intricate harmonies and subtle rhythms created by stringed instruments such as violins, harps, violas, and guitars are beautiful examples of the unification of varying notes and cords, or moods and melodies of the human soul. We each contain variable vibrations within our soul body. The Three of Magic Wands inspires us to play our own symphony with joy and creativity, for this card signifies communication and the joy of self-expression. The three fairies in this card celebrate the muse of the Triple Goddess. The three muses provide clairvoyant insight and intuitive skills.

Questions

Do I doubt my true virtues and skills?

Am I in harmony with the inner symphony of my true talents and inspirations?

How do I allow myself to create joy in my life?

Four of Wands

FOUR OF WANDS

Traditional Meaning

The Four of Wands represents the need to concretize the beneficial influences of creativity in the life of the individual. Here we see the principles of new beginnings that stem from the visions and insights of the previous cards. At this stage they must be planted within the fertile ground of the individual so that a new and vital stage of growth may take root. This card may symbolize a rite of passage or an initiation. In its highest form, this card represents the seeding of new consciousness and the foundation for new beginnings.

Inner Child Cards

Cultivation and gardening require planning, dedication, and foresight. A beautiful garden is the result of one's desire to invoke the presence of beauty and harmony through the co-creative relationship between humanity and nature. Thus, we are able to tangibly experience the interactive relationship between our higher inspirations and the physical world. Similarly, we as human beings must continue to seek greater ways to unite the subtle and invisible forces of the higher mind with the mundane and earthy aspects of daily life. Focus, determination, and hard work cultivate the bright potential yet to blossom in the individual's life. The fairies pictured in this card represent springtime, when new planting takes place and a new season of waxing solar energy and sprouting awaits.

Questions

Am I fully engaged in the process of seeding new potentials within my creative life?

In what way do I engage with the tangible everyday labor toward the birth of new insights and wisdom?

What new inspirations and creative projects am I planting in my life at this time?

Five of Wands

FIVE OF WANDS

Traditional Meaning

The five in any suit represents change and a need to release stagnation or resistance in the area of life that corresponds to the suit and element of the card chosen. In this case, a magic wand represents fire and the need to move freely in the realm of creativity, intuition, and spirituality. If there is strife or an emotional block inhibiting one from expression and inspiration, this card may be an indicator that there is a need to release creative powers in order that a flow of life energy may return to the individual.

Inner Child Cards

In *Inner Child Cards* all the fives represent our highest potentials. In numerology the number *five* represents freedom, creativity, and change. Ultimately, this number and the five-pointed pentagram represent the highest potential for creativity that a human soul can achieve. We must strive to meet that level of excellence, for, like the heavenly stars, we have the potential to shine brilliantly and shower the earth with our light. This beautiful flower fairy is opening the final petal of a bright yellow flower, a symbolic image of our starry origins revealed.

Questions

What aspect of my creative power am I holding back?
How may I meet—with grace and goodwill—the changes and inspirations that are streaming through my life at this time?
I am opening like a fresh spring flower. What part of my life seeks change and what can I do to assist the process further?

Six of Wands

SIX OF WANDS

Traditional Meaning

The Six of Wands signifies victory and triumph for the individual has done so much to become renewed and revitalized in spirit. The flame within the individual burns once again; there has been a breakthrough and the unification of energies has been restored.

Inner Child Cards

The various stages and cycles of nature that ebb and flow throughout the year serve as a potent mirror to humanity. The Six of Magic Wands reveals the marvels of springtime when the first flowers of spring burst upward through the crust of the earth, offering the gift of nature's rainbow to the world. The gentle rain softens the earth to help lighten the labor of nature's birth. The Maypole is an extraordinary symbol created by humanity to imitate the upward and cyclical motion of the marvelous blossoming of spring flowers that bring new life to the earth. The ecstatic victory of nature shines a ray of hope on all of earth's living creatures on May 1st, May Day. All year round, the Six of Magic Wands offers this potential of life force and joy to all.

Questions

My life is a magical dance. I have been blessed with creative renewal and inspiration. How can I best unite with these beautiful blessings at this time in my life?

Do I take time to honor and appreciate nature and the marvels of life?

Seven of Wands

SEVEN OF WANDS

Traditional Meaning

The Seven of Wands signifies a time when one must take responsibility for his or her own power and initiation. One must be fully present and willing to be in contact with the true essence of the soul. There can be no denial. Even if the world around the individual is invalidating, it is best to remain strong with conviction and goodwill—standing up for one's own true identity. This is a time to bare your soul to the world and expose the truest essence of your divinity.

Inner Child Cards

In the Seven of Magic Wands the sweet flower fairy is in complete harmony and communication with the natural world. Open and vulnerable to the forces of higher vibratory influences, she has become a receptacle for energetic healing. She listens to the delicate tone of the flower's message as rainbow-colored butterflies hover above, representing the healing potential of the seven sacred chakras. Within *Inner Child Cards*, we have named this the healing card. Before one is able to stand tall amongst the challenges of the world, it is imperative for the individual to acknowledge the power of love, healing, and compassion that overlights the journey on earth. Therefore, this card signifies a time of personal mastery and receptivity. Allow the force of nature and the elemental kinship with nature to heal you from within.

Questions

Am I aware of the initiation taking place deep within my body and soul?

Do I take time to integrate the healing forces of nature with the busy schedule of my everyday life?

Am I aware of the subtle needs of my physical body?

Is it time to study and research the dynamic power of energetic and vibrational medicine?

Eight of Wands

EIGHT OF WANDS

Traditional Meaning

This card stands for the ability to overcome the hindrances that may stand in our way. It is fast moving and solid at the same time. The essence of the number *eight* denotes skill and mastery and the Wand suit represents the fires of the soul burning with passion and life force. Communication deepens and your ability to stand your own ground with clarity and focus is strengthened. Difficulties of the past are coming to an end while a sense of wholeness abounds.

Inner Child Cards

The Eight of Magic Wands is about energy and one's ability to summon it toward focus and revitalization. A magical moonlit night is the setting for this fairy reunion. Each extends a magic wand into the central flame in order to unify and recharge their light bodies. They represent our need to remain in contact with kindred spirits, to uphold and strengthen our path of destiny, and to boldly ignite the flame of passion in our life. There are times when we must reconnect with vital people, places, or events in order to engage with the essential fire of our inspiration. This card signifies a time to remain true to your own energies unconditionally.

Questions

Am I aware and conscious of the immense skill and mastery that are offered to me at this time regarding my relationship to higher service and healing?

Am I in contact with my kindred friends and associates?

How may I strengthen my circle of support and friendship?

Nine of Wands

NINE OF WANDS

Traditional Meaning

This card signifies a time when latent power has been reawakened within the individual—providing an opportunity to understand the many possibilities that lie ahead. This is a card of inner wisdom. When one is ready and willing to peek into the unconscious, many facets of creativity become visible and possible. The choice remains with every individual. They may remain blocked by the fears and denials of their life or they may enter a new threshold of far-reaching inner and outer opportunities.

Inner Child Cards

Within each of us exists an inner garden of abundant beauty and fertility. There will be times in our life when we have come to the end of a path or road and an opportunity to move into an inviting and rich new experience beckons. At times the opportunity may feel more like an obstacle than a gift. However, it proves beneficial to venture—with trust and gentle wisdom—beyond the limits of one's known path into the regions of the unknown, in order to claim the gift of new consciousness that awaits. Once again, as in the Seven of Magic Wands, we are met with the rainbow-colored butterflies, representing the seven sacred chakras and our higher human potential. Now nine butterflies await the opening of the garden gate so that they may crown the fairy with healing and joy.

Questions

I must trust my inner guidance as never before. I will not hold back. What measures must I take that I may fully trust the unknown journey that lies before me?

My guidance is strong and sure. My dreams speak to me. How may I strengthen my spiritual trust and deepen my relationship with my higher self?

TEN OF WANDS

Traditional Meaning

This card is an invitation. Acknowledge and trust the vitality and life energy that infuses your life. This card represents the culmination of strenuous efforts and deep commitment to move beyond repression and self-denial.

Inner Child Cards

The Ten of Magic Wands is a crowning and celebration for the radiant fairy who has dared to walk through the garden gate into the fertile terrain of new experience. In the previous card, the Nine of Magic Wands, the rainbow-colored butterflies sat upon the garden gate awaiting the opportunity to honor the fairy with a crown of pure white representing rebirth and purity. The beautiful iris represents ultimate creativity, for the healing signature of these vibrant spring flowers is described as the paintbrush of nature. The presence of these beautiful flowers signifies the pursuit of creative and inspirational work. Intuitive forces are very high. A healing has occurred.

Questions

What are my greatest dreams?

Are they attainable?

How can I constructively change my life so that I may rise up and celebrate a life full of joy, happiness, and healing?

Child of Wands

CHILD OF WANDS

Traditional Meaning

In traditional decks, this card is the Page of Wands. The Page is the listener or the receptive one. There is a sun-like quality, for the radiant light of the psyche has been activated and the path toward creative mastery is well on its way to success. The dance of life is directed toward intuitive measures and spiritual studies will be prevalent. This card is more passive than active, although the fire element of the Wand is rarely passive. Focus and clear insight are the key.

Inner Child Cards

The Child of Magic Wands is represented by the Little Prince from the fable written by Antoine de Saint-Exupery. The pathway home to the origins of creativity and spiritual attunement is the key to this card. We all have a special mission in life, and the Little Prince is a reminder that we must remember who we are and why we are given the gift of life if we are to master our destiny.

When this card appears for an individual, it is time to engage with miracles, celebrations, and dreams. The butterfly serves as a magic carpet carrying the Little Prince on a star-lit mission. The path is forever open, above and below, for the earth is delighted to host the various servants of love and light from near and far. Return to your source and fly to your dreams.

Questions

I am ready to proceed forward and find the best ways to fulfill my creative mission in life. How can I achieve this goal?

How do I contact the "home of my soul"?

Do I trust my inner voice?

Seeker of Wands

SEEKER OF WANDS

Traditional Meaning

In the traditional tarot, this card is the Knight of Wands. The energy inspired by increased intuitive abilities and creativity is set free and is unstoppable. One will truly unite with his or her divine mission and the end result will be joyous and healing. All difficult situations will move in constructive directions.

Inner Child Cards

The Seeker of Magic Wands is represented by Dorothy from *The Wizard of Oz*. Unable to jump aboard the magic balloon that she and the Wizard created for the journey to Kansas, Dorothy is now ready to embark on a different kind of journey. She must find her way to the South where she will meet a guide, the Good Witch, who will instruct her how to manifest her own will and find her way back home. It becomes imperative at this stage of the story that Dorothy activate her own ability to return to Kansas—the roots and security she longs to retrieve. Dorothy discovers that the power to get back home was within her own reach all along— in her magic shoes. After a long adventure filled with magic, danger, love, and maturation, Dorothy clicks her heels and cycles home to her family of friends and loved ones. Seekers or knights will always find their way as long as they are intent upon reaching the destination.

Questions

If I persist with intention and vision will I meet my desired end?

What do I most want to achieve in this lifetime?

Am I on the right path?

If not, what might I do to change my course so that I am moving toward a fulfilled destiny?

GUIDE OF WANDS

Traditional Meaning

Guide of Wands

In the past this card was known as the Queen of Wands. The Queen is known for having compassion and ruling gently, for her authority comes from the heart. The Queen of Wands honors the sacred dimensions of the soul and offers a helping hand to all of those blessed by her presence. The Queen of Wands represents feminine energy in action. Her fiery passions offer the potential for great healing for she governs the seven sacred centers of the body known as the chakras. She inspires the muse inside the individual and serves as a mirror that will enable one to see the divine powers of intuition within.

Inner Child Cards

Occasionally we chose to switch the gender in certain cards as a way of showing how the male and female energies can be represented as the animus or anima in archetypes. We all carry the queen, king, child, and princess qualities within our soul. Whether male or female, there will be times in our life when we are called upon to harmonize our inner self and emphasize the focus on more feminine or masculine energies.

The Guide of Magic Wands is represented by the Pied Piper. This guide has an active and masculine archetypal quality for he has accessed his will and come to the rescue of the town of Hamelin that has been infested with rats. With a creative heart intent on restoring the beauty and high energy of this lovely town, the Pied Piper is hired to pipe the rats out of the town by luring them away with the gentle music he plays. When the town officials refuse to pay him for his service, they symbolize the imbalance we have in our world regarding material and spiritual values. As punishment for their greed, the Pied Piper pipes the children into the mountain, into an unknown reality. One lame little boy cannot make it into the mountain before the door closes. He must return to the town as a potent archetype representing the muse unable to fully manifest power in the physical world. The Pied Piper, as the Queen of Wands, is a pure and vital symbol of the creative spirit who seeks to serve through the gifts of one's higher genius.

Questions

How can I best use my creative power in the world?

Do I have the ability to serve the world with heart and soul?

What gifts and talents does the world need most from me?

GUARDIAN OF WANDS

Guardian of Wands

Traditional Meaning

This card is known as the King of Wands. It is the most majestic and masterful card in the tarot regarding the power of higher intuition and spiritual healing. This card mirrors to individuals that they are ready to fully embrace the talents, creative endeavors, and spiritual discipline that they have focused on in the past. Hard work and great ability pay off and one may assume authority in whatever field he or she has focused upon. The King of Wands brings substance to higher visions and represents perfected form where the heart, mind, body, and soul unite. This beauty is reflected in nature, and it is a rare and beautiful thing when the soul of man is able to manifest such beauty and grace.

Inner Child Cards

Raphael, pictured in this card, is the archangel of providence who watches over humanity and offers direction and care to each struggling soul on earth. The name Raphael actually means "God heals," and the first two letters (Ra) are reminiscent of the Egyptian name for the Sun God, Ra. This card offers the ultimate blessing—the sacred omen of light, love, and wisdom. There are many people on the planet who are dedicating their lives to spiritual service. This is a deep commitment of the soul, for one must pay careful attention to what the universe most needs from them. This careful and watchful assessment is achieved when one has responded to a higher calling and is willing to become a true pathfinder—one who lives a joyous life in pursuit of healing and loving others unconditionally. This is the gift of the Guardian of Magic Wands.

Questions

What affirmations am I receiving from spiritual realms of consciousness?
Am I attuned to the subtle powers of personal mastery?
Can I be an intuitive conduit for this energetic light and share this inspiration with the world?

The Swords of Truth

Ace of Swords

ACE OF SWORDS

Traditional Meaning

This is a card that inspires original thinking, intellectual clarity, and brilliant powers of the mind. An ace is an affirmation heralding new beginnings and birth. The upright sword is a representation of truth at its highest level and serves as a tool to cut through illusion, deception, fears, and all mental constructs that inhibit the growth of a new and evolved consciousness.

Inner Child Cards

The sword, at the highest level, represents spiritual will and the power to conquer fear and doubt in the spiritual and earthly realms. Pictured in this card is the moment when King Arthur—as a teenage boy—pulled the magical sword Excalibur from an anvil at a tournament on New Year's Day. He was then acknowledged as the rightful heir to the throne of Britain. The mythology of this story assists humanity in a profound way, for it was not the brute strength of the boy that allowed him to pull the sword from the stone, but the strength of moral conviction and mental empowerment in synchronicity with a higher calling. The Ace of Swords is an indicator of truth and clarity at a soul level as well as a mental one.

Questions

How can I align my heart and head in such a manner that I am in harmony with a universal truth beyond my own limitations and judgments?

What new truths are emerging within my heart?

Am I living my truth?

If not, what must change so that I am in harmony with my inner wisdom?

Two of Swords

TWO OF SWORDS

Traditional Meaning

In the traditional tarot the two swords in the card are often crossed, representing the need to surrender to a decision beyond the intellect. Often a woman is shown, blindfolded, and unable to see the swords before her. This is an indication that she must move away from dry intellectual and rational thoughts and allow the moist undercurrents of her subconscious to open the doors to her intuition. The card can represent peace and tranquillity or offer one the perspective that there is not a wrong or right answer. There are choices. One must learn to choose and discern beyond the scope of fear.

Inner Child Cards

A very important aspect of this card is the representation of the bright Sun setting behind the two crossed swords, for it allows one to observe the circumference of the circle that holds the duality of opposites within it. Opposites are part of the whole picture; without including both aspects, we cannot fully know the bigger picture of any given situation. This is an important piece of information because our minds govern so much of our daily life. Through the Two of Swords we can come to respect the process of decision as being like life fencing—a dance of the soul in which we learn the skill and grace of the mind. Otherwise we may become frozen, fearful, and unable to make decisions.

Questions

What thoughts and ideas stifle my greater judgment and keep me from the freedom of new thought and action?

Is it difficult for me to make decisions?

If so, why?

Do I follow my instincts or my intellect?

In which do I trust the most?

THREE OF SWORDS

Traditional Meaning

This card indicates a time of difficult decision or worry. Perhaps the individual has become trapped in mind games, relationship hardships, or a level of suffering that has penetrated the mind to the extent that one cannot see beyond the scope of the situation. This is a mind trap and the Three of Swords can only bring tension to the individual if this is the case. One has lost touch with the heart or with the all-embracing quality of love that can soothe and clear all wounds of the mind.

Inner Child Cards

The number *three* in numerology signifies joy, communication, and harmony. In the traditional tarot, the Three of Swords is the only *three* card in the Minor Arcana that lacks the message of joy and healing. The *Inner Child Cards* seek to balance the individual by reminding him or her that every situation offers seeds of opportunity and abundance that can sustain the possibility of soul growth. This does not diminish the power of the Three of Swords, but strengthens its vitality and purpose. The highest way to perceive the card is to understand the true essence of the mind. Most often, the mind governs our reality. In a sense, the young maiden is a replica of Rapunzel who must free herself from the inhibiting factors of the tower. In this case she is encased in the stone walls of the castle, yet—like Rapunzel in The Tower card—there is a window with a view of a greater reality awaiting her. She must move beyond the restrictions of her current situation. The young maiden has turned the swords into a musical triangle in order that she may harmonize her situation and meet the gift of the opportunities that lie beyond her mental imprisonment.

Questions

What thoughts are blocking my ability to move beyond the present circumstances that restrict my happiness and joy?

I have the power within myself to merge my mind and thoughts with my heart and feelings. This merging will put me in a state of balance and peace. What measures must I take to fully engage with this possibility?

Four of Swords

FOUR OF SWORDS

Traditional Meaning

This card signals a time when the crisis or opportunity of the Three of Swords has been met with success. This is a stabilizing and fortunate time as the harmonies of the intuitive feeling world have met with the mental constructs of the mind. Whatever seemed hopeless now offers an opportunity for good fortune and peace. However, this card comes with a warning. Do not overlook what might be hidden or buried in the unconscious, for if one does not take time to meditate and bring peace and harmony into all aspects of the situation, repressed mental anxiety could surface and cause further suffering or worry.

Inner Child Cards

At various stages of life we have the opportunity to move beyond the old patterns of thought and move our consciousness toward new and enlightened possibilities, which are portrayed in the Four of Swords by the golden castle in the distance. The wooden raft that the four lads journey upon represents the foundation of current thoughts and projections. Their swords have turned into fishing rods in order that they may extend their understanding to include the deep interior of the unconscious. The inner truth (represented by the stream), accompanied by the desire to understand freedom (the raft), emerges from the watery depths of the past and becomes available as newly established clarity in any given situation.

Questions

In order to maintain a strong foundation of clarity and truth in my life, I must identify the form and constructs that shape my mind and determine whether my current life situation supports further growth and success. Am I paying attention to the undercurrents of my thoughts?

Am I searching for new ways to understand my life and the conditions that surround it?

Five of Swords

FIVE OF SWORDS

Traditional Meaning

This card can represent a situation in which changing circumstances are causing strife and worry in the mind of the individual. If one has neglected to understand the cause of past worry and concern, then this card might call attention to those issues once again. The number *five* cards are about change. If we are not willing to embrace the courage to change rigid thought patterns or projections, this card could indicate a feeling of defeat or despair. However, if we are paying attention to the signals life offers us each day, we may use this card as an indication that there is more to the present situation than meets the eye. It can indicate a need to explore further options.

Inner Child Cards

In *Inner Child Cards*, all of the *five* cards of the Minor Arcana carry the potential for perfected understanding and clarity, for the *five* is a minor version of the upright pentagram that mirrors the divine possibilities of the human being. Although the *five* card of each suit can represent change and perhaps misdirected energies, *Inner Child Cards* seek to remind individuals that they have the chance to empower their lives with the choice of freedom and perfection, energies that emerge from the deeper meaning of the number *five* as well. The young lad pictured in the Five of Swords has discovered something new that lives under the waters of the oceanic mind. As he is perched on a slippery rock formation, it is clear that he must be cautious.

However, his curiosity and willingness to uncover the unseen aspects of the inner world will be rewarded with new understanding.

Questions

I am not afraid to change my opinions and thoughts if this can open and extend my mind to further growth and liberation. What ideas and thought forms have surfaced, allowing me new opportunities to examine the content of my inner mind?

Thoughts create reality. I would like to introduce more freedom and mind-expanding concepts about my reality into my life situations. How can I develop this work further in my everyday life?

Six of Swords

SIX OF SWORDS

Traditional Meaning

This is a card of mental clarity, success, and glory. It signifies one's ability to unify new ideas, and bring forth an all-encompassing vision of ideas and thoughts yet to be realized. It furthers one's ability to be objective and far-sighted so that one is able to see beyond the limiting conditions of old thought patterns and beliefs. The changes that are present in one's life should be communicated and shared with many. This is an exuberant card that celebrates the hard-won results of good relationship and communication.

Inner Child Cards

The bridge that connects the heart and the mind is nothing less than the consciousness of higher understanding and wisdom. True power—the power of love—is evident in this card. The mind has been purified and cleansed; purpose, conviction, and clarity have been established. The card heralds a great toast, a salute, to a unified vision. The heightened mind, symbolized by the swords, is infused with light. The mind is brilliant and full of triumph.

Questions

How do I use my strengths in the area of communication that aid my clarity and focus?

What new truths have I integrated into my daily life?

How are they changing my life for the better?

Seven of Swords

SEVEN OF SWORDS

Traditional Meaning

The number *seven* connects with Trump number VII, The Chariot, and offers perspective and inner guidance. The key is research and self-discovery. Thus, the card signals one's initiation into a greater view of the vast world of imagination, illusion, doubt, or confusion that might be living within the confines of the intellect. Imagination is a great thing as long as one can discern the difference between what is real and what is imagined. At certain times in life, we are fooled by our own inner voice and are unable to clearly detect the difference between our old thought patterns and what we might believe to be higher guidance. The Seven of Swords addresses this issue and offers an astute warning to check twice before coming to final conclusions.

Inner Child Cards

In the busy world we live in, there are times when we must quiet the mind and be still, allowing the more subtle aspects of our psyche to come to the fore. In Inner Child Cards, the mental swords have turned to pens or writing instruments, calling for a time to record or journal one's thoughts in order to objectify them. This helps one to feel secure and confident that the voice within is offering a positive direction in life. The young lad pictured in this card contemplates the reality of a vista yet to be explored, yet he must first understand the meaning of his present situation and current state of mind before venturing into the future.

Questions

Are my perceptions clear?

Do I need a time-out for rest and meditation?

Is it time to purchase or make a journal so that I may record my inner thoughts and ideas?

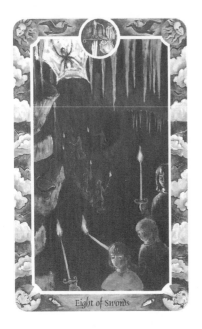

Eight of Swords

EIGHT OF SWORDS

Traditional Meaning

This card signifies a need to develop the skill to travel into the depths of the mind in such a manner that a new foundation will eventually be built. The force and power of the number *eight* supports the energy of transformation at all levels. Individuals may rise to great achievement if they are willing to go with the changing energetics. Traditionally, this card indicates that an individual may be creating too much worry or stress within the mental realm. It is important to check the foundation from which the crisis is stemming and change it.

Inner Child Cards

The spider represents the enigma of the web, which weaves in and out of itself. Our minds are similar. We reshape and recreate our thoughts continuously. The snake, coiled in a figure eight (the symbol of infinity), is the psychic power and life force within. The swords in this card have been changed into torches in order to light the caverns of the mind and illuminate the hidden demons and fears that may be blocking an individual from clear thinking and wise decision making. This is an excellent time to clean the interior of the mind and make way for new and uplifting clarity and information.

Questions

The problems that seem unsolvable now will soon be understood and cleared. What are the deep issues and patterns that block me from being fulfilled and confident with my life?

What three issues seem to prevent me from being free of worry, doubt, and fear? I will write down three things that seem to plague me and choose a tarot card for each one that will show me the way to resolution.

Nine of Swords

NINE OF SWORDS

Traditional Meaning

This card appears when one is fully engaged in old patterns of thought and fear that are worn and outdated. Individuals have the opportunity to move beyond the scope of these old mental constructs as long as they are able to recognize this familiar place of paralysis or inertia that has frozen the fear or worry deep into the caverns of the unconscious. Some people will torture themselves endlessly for having made a poor choice or decision. This self-defeating pattern will be recognized with the appearance of the Nine of Swords and offers the perspective for change and completion in these areas.

Inner Child Cards

When an individual is limited by old patterns and belief constructs, their view of life can be stifled and challenged. The ideas and concepts that we have logged into our bank of memory during a lifetime hold unconscious belief systems that have been programmed since birth. A revolutionary time cycles into our life when it is time to empty the bin, so to speak, and let go of the material of the past that no longer serves the present or the future. With the appearance of this card, we are reminded that our old thought patterns can become like a prison to our soul. Surrounded by the confines of our fears, we often fail to face the parts of ourselves that are in need of healing. The young lad is surrounded by the swords. The dragon (his inner healing journey) stands outside the template of his conscious mind, willing and ready to ally with the boy. When the boy is ready, he will look up, thank the swords for their protection, and dare to move beyond the survival program that has aided him up to this day. He will soon find great delight as he discovers that he is empowered in new and fulfilling ways.

Questions

I am ready to release my old thought forms. I do not have to be a prisoner of limiting thought structures. Do I feel safe when I consider letting go of old fears?

What is required of me?

[Name three magical and beautiful thoughts to replace old thought forms once you have let them go.]

Ten of Swords

TEN OF SWORDS

Traditional Meaning

This card has powerful connotations regarding the deepest and most potent content of the mind. In some decks, this card is connected to insanity or loss of control of the mind. It signifies the final stages of mental organization and reorder before one steps onto the bountiful path of mastery. This is a breakthrough card. When it appears, seek to understand the deepest underpinnings of your thoughts, words, and deeds. The power of language governs manifestation and abundance. It is well worth the effort to expand beyond limits and fears.

Inner Child Cards

Inner Child Cards heralds the Ten of Swords as a potential liberation from the strife of the past. The young lad has had the courage to look up and he has met the dragon (his healing potential) with great success. Now—instead of being encircled by imprisoning images of swords—the boy is placing the final sword of liberation (his new mental clarity and freedom) into the circle of freshly planted thoughts. He is free and vibrant, ready to embark upon the path of mastery.

Questions

What changes about my life as I engage with the newfound freedom from fear and doubt?

Is my mind a clear channel for the expression of higher willpower originating in my soul and spirit?

Child of Swords

CHILD OF SWORDS

Traditional Meaning

In the traditional tarot, this card is known as the Page of Swords. This is the first step toward personal mastery over negating thoughts and patterns. Receptive by nature, the Page is reflective and contemplative. The Page is naïve in some ways, but in other ways he is the wisest of all for he is still infused with innocence. Therefore, the Page is always ready to learn and absorb new information and insight. This is a quality that endears the Page to our hearts. The Page of Swords is still learning about the deeper meaning of truth, and is ready and willing to remove all obstacles and lies from his life. He must first discover what they are and how he can rid himself of the old mental powers that block his progress.

Inner Child Cards

The Page of Swords becomes the Child of Swords. This card is represented by Pinocchio, a wooden puppet, who goes through the initiations of life in order that he may become flesh and blood like his maker, Gepetto. He yearns to incarnate and walk the path of truth. Gepetto is symbolic of our maker or our high self who holds the hologram of consciousness that we strive to attain. Children love Pinocchio because he is so much like them. All human beings make big mistakes as they struggle to fulfill great dreams.

Pinocchio's lessons are ones that we must all experience; they point us toward the true meaning of truth and honesty. The Child of

Swords is ready to engage in the beginning stages of maturation. The ultimate test lies in the ability to discern and prune away the habitual behaviors of the past. With the Child of Swords as an archetypal guide, there is room for improvement and growth, a generous gift still available at this stage of initiation.

Questions

This is a wonderful time to forge plans, look ahead, and begin to see a future opportunity that is available to me. I don't want to block my foresight and vision. Do I create excuses for myself—enabling me to continue pursuing a path that is not for my highest good?

What rationale do I seem to go back to again and again?

What new interests lie before me?

Seeker of Swords

SEEKER OF SWORDS

Traditional Meaning

In older decks, this card is known as the Knight of Swords. This is an active and swift energy card that carries the mental energies forward through whatever has been stagnating, helping one to make decisions and good choices. This card signifies intellectual power, ambition, and goal orientation. One is learning to harness the power of concentration. This card leads one toward the ultimate goal of universal truth and clarity.

Inner Child Cards

The Seeker of Swords in *Inner Child Cards* is represented by the Scarecrow from *The Wizard of Oz,* the first of the three companions that Dorothy meets along the Yellow Brick Road. The Scarecrow represents the power to communicate and offers an understanding that deep inside we have all of the wisdom and intelligence that we need to learn about the world around us. The Scarecrow thought he needed the Wizard to give him a brain. When Dorothy met him he stated: "I don't mind my legs and arms and body being stuffed, because I cannot get hurt. If anyone treads on my toes or sticks a pin into me, it doesn't matter, for I can't feel it. But I do not want people to call me a fool, and if my head stays stuffed with straw instead of with brains, as yours is, how am I ever to know anything?"

As Dorothy and her friends travel down the Yellow Brick Road, they are very powerful archetypal images like the knight in the tarot.

The Scarecrow, like the others, is on a quest, seeking ownership of the true power that lies within him. As he ventures into the various challenges and obstacles along the way, he is able to use his own wits and common sense, and comes to understand his mental gifts and intelligence.

Questions

This is a wonderful time to set a goal and forge ahead with new plans and ideas. What have I been hoping to achieve or accomplish in my life?

What future path can I pave for myself so that I may meet my goal? [Draw a card that will give you a message that will address your new ambitions.]

GUIDE OF SWORDS

Traditional Meaning

Guide of Swords

In the traditional tarot, the Guide of Swords is known as the Queen of Swords. The Queen offers a watery image of the sword suit; the quality of emotion is more present in this card. This card helps individuals to let down the guard of old masks and rational dogmas that keep them from knowing the true source of wisdom lying beneath the surface of external constructs. The Queen's intellectual strength is coupled with deep emotional perspectives. At this stage of maturation, the goals and ambitions of the individual must be aligned with the passions of the heart, for the Queen is the embodiment of compassion and truth.

Inner Child Cards

Inner Child Cards has switched the gender in this card; yet, as in a fairy tale, the feminine aspect of the card is clearly present. In fairy-tale lore, male and female characters represent the inner qualities of the masculine and feminine roles even though they may not be living in the stereotyped gender role. This is a theme that we wish to teach with *Inner Child Cards*. The Queen of Swords represented as Robin Hood portrays the feminine qualities of fairness, love, compassion, and generosity in a male gender role. The leadership of Robin Hood is directed from the heart; however, it is not without great wit and clever foresight. Robin Hood as the Queen of Swords unites a caring heart with a keen mind.

Questions

How can I remain more true to myself through my actions and communications?

I have a great ability to understand the needs of others and to communicate well. How can I best use this gift?

Do I help others with my gift of insight?

GUARDIAN OF SWORDS

Traditional Meaning

In the traditional tarot, the Guardian of Swords is known as the King of Swords. This is one of the power cards of the tarot. The way in which this card is used will identify whether or not individuals are using their power for the good of the whole or for their own gain. The power of thought and the attachment to mental ideas and values can be entrenched within a cultural paradigm that determines whether ideas and concepts are used to sway the masses toward constructive or destructive methods. It becomes a great task for each individual to remain open and receptive to progressive modalities of thought and action. It requires great skill to remain in balance in thought and deed. The King of Swords offers the highest potential for an individual to attain this goal.

Inner Child Cards

The King of Swords has become the Guardian of Swords in *Inner Child Cards*. He is identified as Michael, the angel of truth and will, for he is the personification of spiritual might and willpower. The name Michael actually means, "Who is like God." He attempts to instill in humanity the sense of creative power to manifest goodwill on Earth. Pictured with his winged armor and sword upright, Michael protects and embraces each individual who seeks a life of clarity and focus. The beautiful rose at the base of the sword offers an indication that the truth of God—Michael—is based in love. This love will set humanity free in truth, love, and light.

Questions

Can I free myself from whatever limits my mind and spirit from empowerment, ultimate understanding, and wisdom?
Am I a free agent of divine intelligence?
Is my life an expression of foresight?

The Winged Hearts

ACE OF HEARTS

Traditional Meaning

The Ace of Cups in the traditional tarot represents the gift of love. This card can signify the renewal of a lost love, the possibility of a new love, or—on a personal level—the healing of the heart. It can signify a time in life when one is opening to the expansion of the feeling world and is more in touch with deep-seated emotions. The card will almost always denote a positive affirmation.

Inner Child Cards

As the beautiful winged heart is being lifted upward toward the light of the brilliant sun, there is a triumphant glow in the heavens. When this card appears for individuals, they can be assured that their hard efforts to understand love and make it a conscious attribute in their life are coming to fruition. The glorious winged heart signifies the evolution of unconditional love. All relations are brought to a new level of understanding and the heart radiates forgiveness and trust. This card can represent a time when an individual is experiencing new awareness in the area of childhood memories. Emotional cleansing and renewal are at hand.

Questions

In what area of my life am I learning the most about love?
Do I say "yes" to the love that is pouring into my life? If not, why?

Two of Hearts

TWO OF HEARTS

Traditional Meaning

All occurrences of the number *two* signify balance. Perhaps something is out of balance and needs to be aligned; or an individual may be balancing many situations and the card is a reminder of this. In the Two of Cups, we often see the beautiful union of a male and female. This has been called the marriage card, but it is also connected to the inner union of the feminine and masculine principles.

Inner Child Cards

Here we experience divine union with all levels of emotions and feelings. All is in sweet harmony as the two dolphins jump over the rainbow arch. The rainbow treasure sits at the center of the heart chakra. Both the mermaid and the merman represent devotion and the many facets of color and light that emanate and pour forth from an individual's heart when that person has committed to a unified understanding of unconditional love.

Questions

How is love reflected back to me in my life at this time?

Do I give ample time to explore my emotions and feelings with my partner or the people with whom I am most intimate?

How do I balance the aspects of self and other in my daily life?

Three of Hearts

THREE OF HEARTS

Traditional Meaning

The Three of Cups denotes a time of communication and social interaction that is mutually satisfying to all involved. Shared visions and dreams are a focal point and this card emphasizes the union of hearts. Happiness and celebration abound.

Inner Child Cards

The treasure chest sitting at the floor of the ocean holds the abundant hope that is found in this card. The sea castle in the distance holds a promise of universal abundance. The mermaid and the merman form a circle of radiant hope, like a halo, over the sweet musician, for she is holding within her heart the melody of love that will inspire relationship and the human heart to move to its highest potential of joy.

Questions

Am I in communication with the truest values of love in my life?
Do I allow joy in my life?
What treasures am I discovering about myself that let me feel more creative and inspired?

FOUR OF HEARTS

Traditional Meaning

This card often portrays discontentment and disappointment. The feeling of uselessness or defeat in the matters of emotion and the heart prevail. However, in most decks there is a solution. This is the foundation of the card. If the person in the card will look beyond despair and toward the higher principles of new hope and possibility, then they will see that they are being offered a renewed opportunity.

Inner Child Cards

A forlorn mermaid sits amid the wreckage of her little boat, symbolizing lost hopes and sunken dreams. Dangling upon her arm is her winged heart necklace that has been broken in two. Head down, with eyes covered, she has yet to notice the support and help that's coming to her aid—caring mermaids riding upon the backs of dolphins, often thought of as "the angels of the sea." In time, she will be graced with the love and assistance of the helpers. However, she must open her eyes to the spiritual love and assistance that supports her. Only then will she resolve her broken heart.

Questions

Am I in a relationship or a life situation that restricts me?
Have I opened to the full picture of my circumstances or situation?
Am I grateful for the spiritual abundance and love that surround and guide me each day?

Five of Hearts

FIVE OF HEARTS

Traditional Meaning

In the traditional tarot this card indicates loss; yet there is still hope, for two cups remain standing amidst three fallen ones. This can indicate an inheritance. Perhaps the expectations were too high and one has fallen to disappointment or there is a fear of disappointment. Either way, the person must seek some greater understanding of the situation in order to reach the inner fulfillment of the Six of Cups.

Inner Child Cards

Within the chaos and change of the number *five* the potential for greatness and accomplishment lies hidden. The upright golden star within the mermaid's winged heart is a reflection of the heavenly star above her head. Although she may have been shipwrecked and lost, she has found something splendid in the treasure chest, representing the inner world of her soul. The turtles represent the sturdy foundation from which she will embark upon a new understanding of her situation.

Questions

How can I heal the disappointments that have shaped the inner reality of my life?

Do I acknowledge the golden star that overlights me day and night?

How can I best embrace the essence of inspiration that lives within the depths of my heart?

SIX OF HEARTS

Traditional Meaning

In the traditional tarot this card is a lovely respite from the previous two cards, the Four and the Five of Cups. Finally, with a sense of refreshed appreciation for the love that has filled one's heart once again, the cups overflow with the abundance that true and unconditional love has to offer. This card indicates a rich exchange with those you love and an emotional reward.

Inner Child Cards

The mermaids in the Six of Cups are assisting each other as they emerge fully refreshed and renewed from the depths of the waters or unconscious. As they rise up, they greet the magnificent Sun that warms the soul after a period of inner searching and emotional turmoil. The stork represents the potential for rebirth and fertility in the area of love and emotion.

Questions

What is the best way that I can express my love to the world?
Now that I am conscious of the patterns of the past, how may I deepen my understanding of the law of love?
Do I appreciate the love that governs my life?

SEVEN OF HEARTS

Traditional Meaning

The Seven of Cups represents a time of emotional searching. It is time to still the restlessness of the heart and tend to the unresolved issues surrounding emotions and feelings. The patterns of life reappear, allowing for another, closer look into the greater matters of the heart.

Inner Child Cards

Sitting in the sanctuary of an underwater temple, this quiet mermaid is contemplating the deeper meaning of love. Surrounded by an aura of golden light, she is embraced by the divine presence of clarity and truth. The number *seven* expresses a spiritual quality and the presence of this card indicates the time has come to quiet your inner emotions and listen to the dictates of your higher mind.

Questions

Have I over-taxed my emotions lately?

Is it time for a rest?

Is it time to meditate and peacefully embrace my inner world?

EIGHT OF HEARTS

Traditional Meaning

This card speaks of stagnation and a need for renewal and change. The power of emotion has brought one to a new level of consciousness and the individual must now confront the old fears and emotions that have been stifling. If the flow of change is constant, there will be ample opportunity for new life.

Inner Child Cards

The mermaid and merman are harmoniously brought together in a tantric rhythm that moves and flows with the movement of the deep waters of the ocean. The symphony of sound vibrates a tone of healing that stirs the soul to new dimensions of awareness and unity. The Eight of Winged Hearts represents an unconscious kind of change at a very deep level. One may be experiencing a change of heart or a new understanding of the value of love. An inward call to unity is at hand.

Questions

Are there areas in your life that feel stagnant?
What actions can you take that will ignite a flow of creativity in your life?
Are you ready to revitalize your passions?

NINE OF HEARTS

Traditional Meaning

In the traditional Nine of Cups card, all is harmonious and balanced. The cups are filled and overflow with the abundance of gifts and a blessed feeling of joy that is deeply rooted within the soul. There is a sense of happiness and contentment for the final stages of evolution have manifested within the individual regarding one's understanding of love and compassion. A peaceful resolution is at hand.

Inner Child Cards

The mermaid pictured in the Nine of Winged Hearts is holding a golden urn under a magnificent waterfall, representing the overflowing abundance of her inner life. A vibrant rainbow arches in the background adorned with nine beautiful winged hearts. This is a time to rejoice and return to the wishes and dreams of your heart.

Questions

Are you taking time to rejoice in the eternal spring of your beautiful feelings about life?

Are you remembering to live in joy?

[Remember to hold your arms up like a golden chalice and receive the gifts of love that the universe pours down upon you.]

TEN OF HEARTS

Traditional Meaning

This is a card of deep satisfaction and fulfillment. It is a Tree of Life of the emotions for it heralds the new and renewed imprints of the ancestral past. A new beginning is at hand, yet the passage or initiation that has been completed connects one to the essential core patterns of the original blessings from birth. Freshly awakened, one is able to concentrate on the potentials of the future while simultaneously honoring the roots of love from the past.

Inner Child Cards

This is a card of gratitude. The mermaid has become a blessed vessel of love. Her arms stretched upward, she extends the rainbow's glow from one hand to the next. The tenth winged heart crowns her forehead—opening the channels of pure love to pour through her entire being. Grounded and steadfast, she sits upon the turtle's back, a symbol of earthly riches, and heralds the dawning of love renewed.

Questions

Do I feel deserving of love and abundance?

What do I have to be grateful for in my life?

Am I conscious of the true and pure gifts of love that adorn my inner world?

Child of Hearts

CHILD OF HEARTS

Traditional Meaning

In the traditional tarot, this is called the Page of Cups. The receptive and youthful vitality of this card offers one an opportunity to explore the innocent realms of the heart. This is the first call to mastery as one steps into the terrain of conscious love. This is a beginner's step toward maturation of emotion and inner stability. It beckons a tender salute to the source of love that will eventually set one free from the bondage of fear and denial.

Inner Child Cards

Within *Inner Child Cards*, the Child of Winged Hearts is represented as Goldilocks from the tale of "Goldilocks and the Three Bears." Her innocent gaze into the window of the cottage is a representation of one who is ready and willing to peek into the window of the soul in order to discover what dwells within the home of the unknown parts of ourselves. The Three Bears' cottage symbolizes the nurturing aspects of the home we long to return to. Goldilocks experiments with the bowls, the chairs, and the beds as new and uncertain images evoke her imagination and curiosity. As she rests in the baby bear's bed, she experiences the comfort of a new world of the heart. She is awakened by the surprised bears and scurries back home to the past, carrying within her heart the treasure of the little cottage that she found and explored. Goldilocks is innocent and dear, and her journey into the forest is similar to Little Red Cap's exploration as she ventures off the path to discover new aspects of herself. The Child card of each suit is a minor version of the Fool's Journey.

Questions

How can I enrich and expand the awareness of relationships in my life?

As I explore the unknown dimensions of love in my life, what vital parts of my true needs and security have I uncovered?

Am I in touch with the innocence of true love?

SEEKER OF HEARTS

Traditional Meaning

In the traditional tarot, this is the Knight of Cups. The knights take action. There is a creative ability to take action with one's deep emotions. One is able to unfold the beauty of the heart and offer this gift to the world with noble dignity. This is the pursuit of a higher understanding of love on all levels, whether personal or global, for the court cards represent the journey toward mastery and the power to transcend the personal ego and personality. The realization of these wishes and tasks still lies before the seeker, and must be earnestly sought after.

Inner Child Cards

The Seeker of Winged Hearts is represented by the Tin Man in *The Wizard of Oz*. When Dorothy meets the Tin Man while traveling the Yellow Brick Road, she finds a rather stiff and rusty fellow who has not shed a tear in a very long time. His joints are not oiled; he has been trapped within the confines of his armor suit and he has lost touch with the feeling world. Upon meeting Dorothy he is moved by her kindness and helpful nature. He requests that she oil the joints of his coat of armor so that he might move freely once again. His desire to meet the Wizard of Oz stems from his hope to recover a lost heart and retrieve the virtue of love and emotion. What we find by the story's conclusion is that the Tin Man expresses this kind virtue throughout the story and when it is time to ask the Wizard for a heart, it is clear that the Tin Man has found it within himself.

Questions

How can I seek union with like-minded individuals who share the same vision of love as myself?

How can the interchange of my relationships be enriched?

Do I communicate with the world through my heart or my head?

How can I bring greater balance into my life regarding love and relationship?

GUIDE OF HEARTS

Traditional Meaning

In the traditional tarot, this is known as the Queen of Cups. In all suits, the Queen holds the essence of compassion and love within her majesty. As the Queen of Hearts, she is exalted into a state of universal love and holds the magic solution that will allow us all to find our way back home to the origins of our soul where the truest blessings of forgiveness and healing exist. She is the Rose Queen, the Mother of the World, who represents the unfolding potential of the heart.

Inner Child Cards

The Guide of Winged Hearts is depicted as Glinda, the good witch of the South in *The Wizard of Oz*. After failing to board the great balloon with the Wizard, Dorothy and her companions must find another way home. They journey to the South where Glinda resides in a beautiful castle. As they enter the big room of the castle, Glinda sits on a splendid throne of rubies. Her kindness and love embrace Dorothy and her friends and each one of them is offered a wish regarding their future. Dorothy, of course, wishes to return home to Kansas. Glinda says: "The silver shoes have wonderful powers. And one of the most curious things about them is that they can carry you to any place in the world in three steps, and each step will be made in the wink of an eye. All you have to do is knock the heels together three times and command the shoes to carry you wherever you wish to go."

We all long to return to the origins of our true home—the place of unconditional love that holds our divine essence and unique creative mission intact. Glinda represents that stage in our life when one seeks the true path of the heart. In order to go home to the soul, we must first follow the guidance of our higher self that illuminates the path toward unconditional love.

Questions

What do the silver shoes represent to me at this time?

If I were to click my heels together three times where would I wish to go?

Do I know my way home?

Is my heart safe and embraced by the guidance of my higher self?

GUARDIAN OF HEARTS

Guardian of Hearts

Traditional Meaning

In older decks, the Guardian of Hearts is the King of Cups. The Holy Grail is the chalice of divine healing and love, and the King of Cups is the keeper of this potential. He has fully merged with the compassion of the Queen of Cups and it's now his task and honor to bring form and foundation to the manifestation of love on earth. This is the stage in life where individuals are seeking harmony with their own authority to give and receive love with great understanding and respect. The King is a master. This is the final step the individual takes toward the alchemy of spiritual love.

Inner Child Cards

In *Inner Child Cards*, the King of Cups is represented as the archangel Gabriel, who is embodied as a beautiful angelic mermaid, Gabrielle. The archangel Gabriel reveals divine messages to humanity. Gabriel literally means "Hero of God," one who brings joyous tidings to the faithful as well as mercy to those who have fallen prey to their lower instincts. As the fateful judge, Gabriel helps align those in need of connecting the beauty of the soul with the body. This angel was the ambassador who came to Mary, declaring that her child would be the messiah long awaited by the Jewish people. Gabriel blows the trumpet of rebirth, asking human beings to rise up and embrace the universal code of unconditional love and healing.

Questions

I realize that I am the master of my emotions. What areas of my life pull me away from divine love and self-healing?

Am I in harmony with my greater community?

Do I have appropriate outlets and opportunities to give my love to the world through service?

If not, how can I change this so that my heart is radiant with sharing and joy?

The Earth Crystals

Ace of Crystals

ACE OF CRYSTALS

Traditional Meaning

This card symbolizes inner and outer success. The ace is always a gift. In this suit, it represents the gift of earthly abundance and material reward. There is a beautiful harmony between body and soul, and the new birth of a higher consciousness is available. This consciousness enables one to bring visions into manifestation. This card can signify the birth of a child, a new enterprise, or the establishment of concretized ideals.

Inner Child Cards

A magnificent crystal has been uncovered by a hardworking gnome and its rays of light create a brilliant rainbow across the heavens. In *Inner Child Cards*, this card is called the Ace of Crystals. There are stages in our life when we are led back toward the deepest treasures of our true self. At times this journey may be focused on the emotional, spiritual, or mental level; however, this card indicates that the journey home is physical. This card heralds a time when a new birth cycle has arrived and what is uncovered is the gem of incarnation. It is now time to fully embody and engage with the material riches of life—be it new vocation, relationship, family, or creative abundance. Like the little gnome in this picture, you have worked very hard and have now arrived at a point of reward.

Questions

I am ready to live a life that is inwardly and outwardly rich and abundant. How can I position myself in my daily life so that I may offer and receive these gifts?

Do I believe in my abundance?

What areas of my life would I like to make richer?

Two of Crystals

TWO OF CRYSTALS

Traditional Meaning

In the traditional tarot, this card indicates change. Something in the physical world is shifting and seeking a new balance or equilibrium. It asks that we do not become fixated on the current conditions of life. It reminds us to resist the tendency to become stagnant and inert through our attachment to the permanent state of affairs governing our life. This card will appear as a signal or a warning: do not become too attached to the material world; seek balance; take good care of your physical health.

Inner Child Cards

The Two of Crystals reveals two little children, a gnome girl and boy, playing the game of seesaw, a game that requires balance and harmony between two people in order for the game to go well. Fair play and cooperation are the integral aspects of this playground game, for if one person decides to make a move out of accordance with the balance of the beam, either person may be seriously injured. Have you ever slammed down to the ground while on a seesaw? It doesn't feel good. The same applies to life. When we are out of balance inwardly or outwardly with the conditions of our life, we often feel slammed or struck down, quickly and abruptly. When this occurs, we are usually out of balance with the flow of our life and it is time to readjust the game.

Questions

What adjustments must I make in my life in order that I may bring greater balance and stability into my current life situation?

Am I taking good care of my physical health with enough rest, good food, and creative outlets?

If not, what must I do in order for my life to return to a state of balance and harmony?

THREE OF CRYSTALS

Traditional Meaning

Often this card depicts an "architect of the higher worlds" building a stained glass window in a cathedral. Three windows are displayed in a triangular form, representing body, soul, and spirit. This pyramid of unity guides the aspirant onward. One's whole being is engaged with a pure and creative drive that can only reap positive benefit. There is a representation of energies coming together in harmony and perfect alignment, allowing for abundant result.

Inner Child Cards

Within *Inner Child Cards,* the unity in this card is represented by three children playing. The number *three* represents community, communication, and joyful reunion with family and friends. The three children are playing the game of jump rope. This game, like the seesaw game in the Two of Crystals, requires cooperation and balance; however, in this scenario, another player is added. These players are not attached to a steady beam—like the seesaw—that dictates the harmony of the game. Instead, this game includes the flowing unpredictability of a jump rope. This card indicates that more individuality is present and there is more choice among the players to create harmony and a successful outcome of the game. The Three of Crystals is a positive signal, especially as it relates to the affairs of joyous celebrations and creative outcomes.

Questions

It is time to engage myself totally in the creative projects that I have begun. What would I like to achieve through my creative efforts? What must I focus on in order to fulfil this dream?

Am I willing to be joyously united with and accepted by my community and friends?

Four of Crystals

FOUR OF CRYSTALS

Traditional Meaning

The Four of Pentacles is a card of character and discipline. It indicates the reward of hard work and focus. The sturdy foundation of willful action and dynamic enterprise pays off. The power indicated in this card must be rooted in strong principles, determination, and high values, for it is associated with the material world and includes a strong relationship to money, land, career, and ownership of personal empowerment. This is a card of building a solid form that is orderly and organized. One must be careful of rigidity when this card appears. Let freedom and form unite.

Inner Child Cards

Four sturdy gnomes are busy at work in the Four of Crystals. The tree house represents the sturdy and rooted foundation on which the gnomes build their house. With a strong plan intact, the busy group engages in an ambitious effort to manifest and bring to earth the vision or archetypal blueprint of the little tree house. Whether it is a house, a course of study, an artistic pursuit, or a new life plan, the Four of Crystals prompts you to build your dreams.

Questions

I am ready and willing to become more engaged in the dynamic task of building my life into a realized dream. What efforts must I put forward if I am to manifest my highest ideals?

Am I comfortable with my own power?

What am I building?

Five of Crystals

FIVE OF CRYSTALS

Traditional Meaning

This card indicates a change on the physical plane. Perhaps we have not finished our plans, have a habit of quitting or letting things go before they manifest, or we fear the call to change. This card can indicate worry or concern for money, health, and resources. Ultimately, it signifies a point of chaos that often precedes a creative change or triumph. Traditionally this card has indicated poverty. As this is an earth suit and represents the physical plane, the poverty is usually interpreted to mean money problems or lack of material resources. However, if one looks more deeply into the situation, one may find that the poverty is within the idea realm of the human being and that one must search deeply and sincerely for a way to undo the bindings of old thought forms that live within the body memory. It can be very empowering for an individual to realize that the material world will, in fact, manifest according to beliefs and body memory. The Five of Pentacles is a radical call for change and unfolding.

Inner Child Cards

The number *five* is magic. In *Inner Child Cards*, the number *five* cards hold the potential for blossoming and creativity. When human beings master the ability to unite freedom and form into actual manifested ideals, they have cornered the ability to live to the highest potential of the number *five*. *Five* not only represents change; it is also the power to illuminate the potential of perfection. In the previous card, the busy gnomes are intent on building and manifesting a tree house. In the Five of Crystals, the papa gnome puts the final touches on the stained glass window. One does not have to walk solemnly past the stained glass window with back bent forward in impoverished despair as in traditional card representations. Indeed, one may instead build and re-create the window to reflect the true magic that resides within the human potential. One may become a reflection of the colorful and multi-faceted stained glass window.

Questions

There may be a decision to be made in my life at this time. What changes are necessary in order that I may live a more creative life? What final touches am I adding to my life in order that it may be complete and rich?

Why do I have trouble finishing tasks and fulfilling commitments?

Six of Crystals

SIX OF CRYSTALS

Traditional Meaning

The Six of Pentacles signifies success. Diligent efforts have now established a plateau from which one may count one's blessings. This card often assures a successful outcome of any enterprise. The highest potential for manifestation is present and every detail must be discerned in order that the greatest plan may be achieved. In the world of form and order, there is no better card—other than the Queen and King of Pentacles—to receive than this one. It is a gift.

Inner Child Cards

The gnomes in the Earth Crystal suit represent the atomic structure of the material plane as it relates to the body of the human being. In nature there are many levels of elemental energy, each of which has a distinct part to play in the development of creation. At this juncture of personal growth, the Six of Crystals denotes a time when the soul is ready to incarnate at the highest level and achieve great things. There would be no room for procrastination, laziness, or repetition of mistakes. This is an awakened time within the individual. The sturdy gnomes have climbed long and hard to get to the plateau of the mountain. Each earnest gnome will be rewarded with the gift of a snowflake—containing the unique pattern of his destiny.

Questions

Success involves strength and conviction in order to stay on a path of joy and fulfillment. What inner convictions and depths am I being asked to explore in order that I may understand my higher destiny?
I am ready to succeed. What is my highest path of service?
Am I consciously creating this path of service and success in my life at this time?

Seven of Crystals

SEVEN OF CRYSTALS

Traditional Meaning

The number *seven* in all Minor Arcana cards is a call for a time of inner research. The way in which we explore and meditate upon inner virtues depends on the governing suit. In an earth suit—represented as pentacles, coins, discs, and crystals—the *seven* leads one toward a deep introspection into the blocks and limiting conditions that may be causing worry or hesitation about success and material accomplishment. One must ask the important question: "What does success really mean to me and how am I manifesting it in my present-day life?" The Seven of Pentacles may warrant a time of rest and patience. This is not a time to push forward without the inner wisdom to know what you are seeking to accomplish. The Seven of Pentacles suggests that an individual take the time to research these important life questions concerning success and earthly attainment.

Inner Child Cards

There are times in our life when outer conditions seem harsh and perhaps frozen within an old pattern. We often feel this way when life's demands are fierce and our experiencing of the warmth of "soul pleasure" has decreased. At this crucial time, when life seems to be pressing on us on the physical plane, we may need to pause for deeper reflection on what is truly essential in life. We may have all the riches we need in the world; however, unless we are connected with the vital essence of the heart, we may be out of touch with the true meaning of our destiny. The lovely gnome girl's action of lighting a candle represents the need to reconnect with the inner light. At this stage of development on the path of the Earth Crystal suit, one is busy achieving great rewards in life. The Seven of Crystals represents a time of quiet sanctuary where the balance of the inner and the outer world reaches harmony. This may be a calling to the individual to take a little rest and re-ignite the flame within.

Questions

My ability to strive onward with material gain and success has come to a crossroad. What must I look at deeply within myself in order that I may regain balance and strength?

Am I getting enough rest?

Do I take the time to visualize my dreams and creative fulfillment?

What new actions must I take in order to balance my busy outer life with the peace and tranquillity of my soul?

Eight of Crystals

EIGHT OF CRYSTALS

Traditional Meaning

This is a card of endurance and hard work resulting in success and increasing self-esteem. The individual must be willing and able to expend a tremendous amount of energy toward goals and long-range potentials. *Eight* is a double manifesting number as it is 4+4 , denoting double work, focus, and clarity. The potential for beauty and happiness is near, yet the individual must remain devoted to a focused path of inner strength and truth. Personal empowerment will endure as long as the individual is courageous and honest.

Inner Child Cards

Practice makes perfect. It is one thing to be sufficient at something; it is another to become masterful. In observing the beautiful and stunning artwork of the Renaissance period, we have a glimpse of the masterful works of focus and precision that were central during that phase of history. It is apparent that much of the work and effort was created in tandem with a higher inspiration—one that fostered the individual's ability to harmonize the invisible tapestry of inspiration with material skill and discipline. The Eight of Crystals is a blossoming forth of this potential. Its key message is focus, beauty, and clarity, with the reward of personal abundance.

Questions

The power and strength that is manifesting within me is like a beautiful blossom of light. What can I do in my life at this time to clarify my work and aspirations?

What masterful projects and ideas am I embarking upon?

Is my life in order so that I may attain my highest achievement?

Nine of Crystals

NINE OF CRYSTALS

Traditional Meaning

This card is endowed with grace and harmony for the attributes of hope, faith, and optimism are indicated. The number *nine*, which is a completion number, suggests that something marvelous will continue to transpire as long as the individual is able to believe in the works of the divine and the power of love as a means to attract abundance. The highest task life sets out for us is to realize our greatest gifts and talents and utilize them in the most creative way possible. The Nine of Pentacles asks us to look at our real accomplishments and sort out what is useful and what is not. This card prepares one for a great transformation in the Ten of Pentacles. In a simple way, this card asks individuals to get their house in order and make way for the new.

Inner Child Cards

The Christmas symbols in the Nine and Ten of Crystals are not to be taken literally. The mythology of Christmas is a powerful metaphor that is chosen to portray birth, abundance, light, and earth celebration. In this card, a mama gnome is reading a Christmas Eve story to the little girl while many wishes, secrets, hopes, and dreams stir her soul. The potential for a great visit is in the air. This visit—mythically portrayed in this card as Saint Nicholas—is the manifestation of good intention and a commitment to hope and faith. If you believe in something with all your heart, it is more likely to unfold in a positive way.

This is the law of manifestation. The Nine of Crystals is the gateway into the mastery of abundance. Remember, the more you give out love, the more it will return to you. Prepare yourself, at the highest level, for abundance, and your dreams will come true.

Questions

What are my most fervent dreams and hopes?
Do I have a grand plan for the next phase of my life?
Am I being shown the signs that a new and progressive understanding of the laws of manifestation are gestating within?
Am I in harmony with my ultimate goal?

Ten of Crystals

TEN OF CRYSTALS

Traditional Meaning

This is the card of wealth. A boundless treasure may be brought forth into the world as a result of hard work, faith, and a proper balance between the spiritual and material plane. The riches inherent in the Ten of Pentacles are manifested outwardly and often depict a time in life when individuals may share this great benefit with others. One must always evaluate the way in which they use this great blessing. It is beneficial to use the power of the Ten of Pentacles in service and goodwill to the planet.

Inner Child Cards

Once again we have a scene of Christmas. This time it is Christmas night after all of the presents have been unwrapped and the stockings have been filled abundantly. The story of Christmas is not represented in this card to indicate Christmas from a Christian point of view, but as a theme or metaphor of goodwill and blessings contained in the myths and celebrations of all cultures. Christmas is chosen as a symbol of abundant happiness and new beginnings. Papa gnome lights the yule log while little gnome children gaze at the treasures left in the night by Saint Nicholas. This is a time of celebration and community sharing. Offer your gifts to the world.

Questions

I have attracted an abundant life. I realize that I have created a life filled with treasures. What are these treasures and can I fully recognize the bounty of my blessings?

If not, what stands in my way of embodying the abundance of which I dream?

My internal riches are reflected by my outer world. I have many things to be grateful for.

[Make a list of all of your blessings and hold it to the light. Acknowledge these gifts and share them with the world.]

Child of Crystals

CHILD OF CRYSTALS

Traditional Meaning

In the traditional tarot, this card is called the Page of Pentacles. It represents a time when one is gathering new materials and plans for the next phase of life. It is not an active time; in fact, its energy is more reflective and contemplative. The earth suit represents practical, grounded, and tangible attributes that are granted and mirrored to the individual. Of all four suits, this one calls forth a momentum of physical manifestation and application toward one's goals. The court cards appear when one is ready to engage with the real stuff of life's offerings. The Page of Pentacles marks the beginning point of masterful rewards and a life accomplished.

Inner Child Cards

In *Inner Child Cards*, the Page of Pentacles becomes the Child of Crystals, represented by Mark Twain's delightful character Huck Finn. The adventures of Huck Finn involve his wit and innocence combined with a sense of mischief and risk. As we venture into the higher terrain of our climb in life, we come face to face with the childlike ways in which we have perceived the world. Some of them are useful and some well worn. Our task is a poignant one, for we must find a way to remain innocent and open and, at the same time, to be discriminating and disciplined. As the proverbial vagabond boy, Huck Finn often symbolizes our youthful folly that leads to a fork in the road. We are at the beginning stages of new growth and consciousness. We may circle back to this point many times, each time gaining new understanding of our life's adventure. As Huck dips his fishing rod into the pond, he ponders the day's activities and the way in which he will continue to live and learn. This is the same for an individual who receives this card. Live, make mistakes, learn from them, and carry on. The adventure of life is a never-ending lesson.

Questions

This is a time when mastery and skill are required. What can I do to prepare myself for the coming experiences that will help to shape my future?

What am I gestating within the deep parts of my heart?

What am I ready to manifest?

What powerful lessons have I learned that teach me the laws of truth and right action?

Seeker of Crystals

SEEKER OF CRYSTALS

Traditional Meaning

The Knight of Pentacles is a card of action and precision. It is time to move forward in a practical and pragmatic fashion, clearing the way for the goals you have worked long and hard to achieve. It takes great courage to move up and claim the power of this card. This is an earth suit; therefore, the metaphor of flowers blossoming and new shoots springing vibrantly up from the ground is valid. Knights are often seen on horses moving swiftly, like the wind, carrying messages and service to those in need. Now is the time to enter the realm of realism, to ground energies, and to carry out plans. The Knight of Pentacles is unshakeable. The call within to persevere with plans and new ideas is anchored deeply.

Inner Child Cards

The Knight of Pentacles has now become the Seeker of Crystals represented as the Cowardly Lion in *The Wizard of Oz*. Upon meeting Dorothy, the Lion acts tough and bold, roaring out a frightening sound that surprises Dorothy and her companions. However, when Dorothy faces the Lion with her own will and admonishes him for his rude behavior, he begins to cry and run away. This is a very good example of one who uses outer power as a way of protecting himself with a false identity. In order for the Lion to learn how to truly behave with courage and honor, he must face the real task of defending from his heart. As his love and support grow for the group, especially Dorothy—whose character is the anima of the group—he finds that he does possess true and virtuous strength within. From that place of inner dignity, the Lion learns how to be in true service. This is the highest path of the knight—a path with heart.

Questions

My personal power and confidence stem from the source of my true self. What must I do to fully realize my potential as an earth steward? What qualities must I fully ground and stabilize in order for my leadership and world service to take hold in a new way?

I need to let go of false personal illusions of power. What new parts of my character can I bring forward and share with the world with goodwill and a noble heart?

GUIDE OF CRYSTALS

Guide of Crystals

Traditional Meaning

This card is known as the Queen of Pentacles and is a lesser representation of The Empress in the Major Arcana. She embodies the principles of the love that flows through her heart and the abundance that emanates through her relationship to nature and the stars, and through her reverence for the physical body. She is generous, kind, and deeply understanding, for her wisdom is connected to the earth's stable and constant source of goodness. She is secure and helpful to those in need; she carries an essence of the Divine Mother. The Queen is exalted in the Pentacles suit. She is Earth Mother, Queen Sophia, the birther of all potentials. She is a treasure to behold.

Inner Child Cards

The mythology and tradition of Christmas offer another kind of giving saint to the archetypal world besides baby Jesus. It is interesting that the baby Jesus is more of a spiritual provider, a giver of love and sanctuary from an esoteric viewpoint, whereas Saint Nicholas is the embodiment of generosity and abundance. Children who grow up with Saint Nicholas as a part of childhood lore are urged to hold a dream within their hearts in order that their hopes reveal themselves in the magical morning hours. In *Inner Child Cards*, the Queen of Pentacles is represented by Saint Nicholas, a real, living person of the fourth century who was famous for his holiness, miracles, and kindness. He came to be the patron saint of storm-ravaged sailors, prisoners, and children. He is pictured offering a blessing—much like The Wizard or The Hierophant in the traditional tarot—for he is a jubilant blend of the spiritual and material aspects of humanity that bestow blessings upon us all.

Questions

I seek to understand the power of love and its application in everyday life. The more love and generosity I offer to the world, the more joy I feel in my heart. Am I taking good care of my health and well-being in order that I may be an instrument of goodwill and healing on the planet?

How can I be more generous with my gifts and remain centered and well-balanced within myself?

Guardian of Crystals

GUARDIAN OF CRYSTALS

Traditional Meaning

Majestic, bountiful, dignified, and wealthy are adjectives that refer to the King of Pentacles. Like The Emperor in the Major Arcana, the King of Pentacles is radiant with success and earthly power. However, as in all power cards, the way these characteristics are offered to the world is crucial. This magnificent card must be looked at with great discretion. Is the King satisfied with all of this earthly pleasure without caring or serving the community at large? Is he greedy or is he a citizen of high honor who offers the world a greater understanding of what it is to be abundant and blessed with earthly pleasure and comfort? The King and Queen of Pentacles live with great joy when they have found the path of service to accompany the riches they have gained. This is an apex card in the tarot. When it appears, it is important to review the standards by which you live your everyday life and how you share your resources with the rest of the world.

Inner Child Cards

Gaia, the Earth Mother, represents the King of Pentacles within *Inner Child Cards*. She holds the globe of Earth in her loving hands for she knows that she is the Guardian of the Earth and she must protect, guide, and love all the beings and nature of the planet. "Earth" contains the same letters as "heart," signifying that Earth is a planetary school of love incarnate. We are all divine and, in our quest to heal, we look to teachers and guides to assist us along the way. Gaia serves as an archetypal guide, embracing our divinity in all that we do, assuring us a higher path toward the redemption of love and healing. She reminds us that we are not separate from the flowers, trees, stars, and animal life that surround us each day. The reverence of the temporal and spiritual worlds flourishes with the guidance of Gaia. Love heals all.

Questions

I have been blessed in many ways. How may I share the bounty of love and abundance that has graced my life with those around me?
What true gift do I wish to share with the world?
Am I able to have faith in this great blessing or do I doubt my inner and outer wealth?

Bibliography

Bettelheim, Bruno. *The Uses of Enchantment: The Meaning and Importance of Fairy Tales*. New York: Vintage Books, 1977.

Case, Paul Foster. *The Tarot: A Key to the Wisdom of the Ages*. Richmond, VA: Macoy Publishing Company, 1947.

Fabricius, Johannes. *Alchemy: The Medieval Alchemists and their Royal Art*. London: Diamond Books, 1994.

Gad, Dr. Irene. *Tarot and Individuation: Correspondences with Cabala and Alchemy*. York Beach, ME: Nicolas-Hays, Inc., 1994.

Haich, Elisabeth. *The Wisdom of the Tarot*. Santa Fe: Aurora Press, 1984.

Hall, Manly P. *An Encyclopedic Outline of Masonic, Hermetic, Qabbalistic and Rosicrucian Symbolical Philosophy: Being an Interpretation of the Secret Teachings Concealed within the Rituals, Allegories and Mysteries of all Ages*. Los Angeles: Philosophical Research Society, Inc. 1977.

————. *The Secret Teachings of All Ages*, Diamond Jubilee Edition. Los Angeles: Philosophical Research Society, Inc., 1988.

Jung, C.G. *Psychology and Alchemy*. Princeton, NJ: Princeton University Press, 1993.

Levi, Eliphas. *Transcendental Magic: Its Doctrine and Ritual (1910)*. Kila, Mont.: Kessinger Publishing Co., 1942.

Line, Julia. *Discover Numerology: Understanding and Using the Power of Numbers*. New York: Sterling Publishing Company, 1993.

Meyer, Rudolf. *The Wisdom of Fairy Tales*. Hudson, NY: Anthroposophic Press, 1988.

Taylor, Thomas. *The Theoretic Arithmetic of the Pythagoreans*. York Beach, ME: Samuel Weiser, Inc., 1983.

Tolkien, J.R.R. *The Fellowship of the Ring: Being the First Part of The Lord of the Rings*. New York: Houghton Mifflin Company, 1994.